MAKING SENSE OF PHONICS

The Hows *and* Whys

ISABEL L. BECK

THE GUILFORD PRESS
New York   London

I want to acknowledge my many university students, who have shared their dilemmas with me and raised important questions about their students over the years; and Linda Kucan, whose urgency that the material that follows be made widely available propelled me to write this book, and whose thoughtful and precise editing helped me to complete it.

© 2006 The Guilford Press
A Division of Guilford Publications, Inc.
72 Spring Street, New York, NY 10012
www.guilford.com

Printed in the United States of America

This book is printed on acid-free paper.

Last digit is print number: 9   8   7   6   5   4   3   2

Library of Congress Cataloging-in-Publication Data

Beck, Isabel L.
    Making sense of phonics: the hows and whys / Isabel L. Beck.
        p.   cm. — (Solving problems in the teaching of literacy)
    Includes bibliographical references and index.
    ISBN 1-59385-257-6 (paper); ISBN 1-59385-268-1 (hard)
    1. Reading—Phonetic method.   2. Reading (Elementary)
I. Title.   II. Series.
    LB1573.3.B43   2006
    372.46′5—dc22
                                                    2005019694

MAKING SENSE OF PHONICS

SOLVING PROBLEMS IN THE TEACHING OF LITERACY
Cathy Collins Block, Series Editor

For those I taught and learned from:

My first-grade students
The sergeants
My children, Elizabeth and Mark

ABOUT THE AUTHOR

Isabel L. Beck, PhD, is Professor of Education in the School of Education and Senior Scientist at the Learning Research and Development Center, both at the University of Pittsburgh, Pennsylvania. She was a public school teacher before starting her career at the university. Dr. Beck's work has been acknowledged by awards from the International Reading Association, the National Reading Conference, and the American Federation of Teachers. *Bringing Words to Life: Robust Vocabulary Instruction*, a book she published with her colleagues Margaret G. McKeown and Linda Kucan (Guilford Press, 2002), has become an education best seller.

CONTENTS

PROLOGUE

Over the years, I have developed several instructional strategies for teaching word-level knowledge and skills to children learning to read. Some of the strategies were developed by tinkering with existing ones, others by making an existing strategy more explicit and systematic, and others by combining two strategies. I did this work for several reasons: my firsthand observations of children having difficulty in the course of learning to decode, the requests of my master's-level students for specific suggestions in overcoming problems they saw young readers encountering in word recognition, the development of my own children's literacy skills, and my experiences teaching noncommissioned officers to read. Not too long ago, I wrote a chapter about those experiences (Beck, 1998), and because they were so influential in developing the instructional approaches that will be presented in this book, I have adapted that chapter for presentation here.

I started my reading education career as a first-grade teacher. Subsequently, I taught third-, fourth-, and fifth-grade students. My last teaching experience in public schools was as a kindergarten teacher. In addition, two other practical experiences were enormously important to the development of my understanding of reading: one was teaching noncommissioned officers who did not know how to read at an army camp in Arkansas. The other was watching and interacting with my two children in the course of their literacy development. Additionally, I became very interested in reading research when I started working as a part-time research assistant at the Learning Research and Development Center (LRDC) at the University of Pittsburgh.

It was at LRDC that I discovered some psychological research and theory on reading that addressed some curiosities that had emerged from my experience with first graders as well as with the sergeants. What first got my attention was that some of the psychologists who were writing articles on reading had never taught anyone to read, yet they were able to describe phenomena that I had observed as a teacher of reading. That made me really curious. While studying the psychological literature on reading, I became fascinated with some potential explanations for the real-world phenomena that I had witnessed in students' attempts to learn to read. That fascination was so compelling that I decided to pursue a PhD.

Although my longest and most sustained research has involved reading comprehension and vocabulary development, I've never given up my study of and interest in beginning reading. And so, as I already mentioned, the purpose of this Prologue is to relate my multifaceted experiences in reading to the instructional procedures presented in this book. To do so, I'm going to speak to you in two voices: a personal voice to describe my own experiences and an analytical voice to connect those experiences to reading research. The typeface will cue you about which voice I'm using: *italics* for the personal voice, and regular type for the analytical voice.

TEACHING READING IN FIRST GRADE

My first-grade teaching experiences were in southern California and on the east coast in an urban school district. That there were forty children in each of those classes may tell you how long ago it was. Both classrooms were similarly arranged: the focus in each room was the "reading circle," about 10 little chairs in a semicircle in front of a pocket chart; there were also a library corner with pillows, illustrated color words and days of the week along the borders, class-developed experience charts on a large stand, individually dictated and illustrated little books, and many other such enduring first-grade paraphernalia and props. My desk was in a corner. On one side was an ever-changing collection of such classics as Make Way for Ducklings *(McCloskey, 1941) and* The Story about Ping *(Flack & Weise, 1933), which I read to the children. On the other side of my desk were the Dick and Jane teachers' manuals (Gray, 1952)—dog-eared, clipped, and book-marked.*

Let me tell you a little about those Dick and Jane teachers' manuals. When I started my student teaching in a first-grade in the last semester of my senior year, I knew a lot about children's literature and about reading to children. I knew something about the development of young children and had learned from instructors who exemplified an attitude of kindness and respect for them. As for reading and writing, I knew about developing experience charts, labeling children's drawings, and taking dictation. But, from my critic teacher during student teaching, I learned the most useful thing of all: I learned how to follow the Dick and Jane teachers' manuals.

So, when I entered my very own first-grade classroom in southern California with the sobering responsibility of teaching 40 children to read, I felt enormous relief in finding the Dick and Jane manuals in the cupboard. Those manuals were not only a source of great comfort, they were also a source of great wisdom. I did virtually everything they suggested. We finished the "readiness" book and went on to the first preprimer. Almost all the children were learning to read. That is, they could read the words in the first preprimer. Reading the second preprimer didn't go quite so well. It seemed that several children were forgetting words they used to know and just guessing at new words by saying old words. So I made flashcards for the words and figured out game-like ways to make recognizing the words more interesting.

At about this point, the teacher's manual presented activities for teaching beginning sounds. The manual suggested putting a B on a piece of chart paper and having the children bring in pictures of things that begin with B. Over the weeks, C charts, M charts, S charts, and the like were developed. The children enjoyed bringing the pictures in, and I did what the manual told me to do: I'd ask the students what was the same about the pictures, and they told me that the names of the things all began with the letter B.

As we reached the last pages of the third preprimer, however, it was quite clear that this time more than a few children were forgetting words they used to know. How was that possible? How could they know a word and then not know it? And it didn't get better with the primer: in fact, it got worse. Even more children misread words they used to know, and they weren't remembering new words. After that year in California, I came east and taught first-grade again. This time I was with 40 first graders in a large urban environment. Despite the differences in geography, the reading difficulties of the children were the same as those experienced by my California students.

At the end of those 2 years, there was good news, not-so-good news, and bad news. The good news was that about 50 of those 80 children were developing into good readers. The not-so-good news was that about half of the remaining 30 were kind of shaky readers. They could read target materials adequately, but they didn't seem to have much confidence. The bad news was that, of the remaining 15, most were in trouble. Some got in trouble earlier, some later. Some seemed to forget words right from the start, after 15 or 20 words had accumulated; others didn't forget words until well into the second and third preprimers, when perhaps 70 or 80 words had accumulated.

ANALYSIS OF TEACHING READING IN FIRST GRADE

Why did some of those children misread words they used to know and just guess at new words? Somewhere along the line, probably soon after I had discovered reading research and become more analytical, I became aware that as the word corpus grew larger in the Dick and Jane readers, the misreading index grew. How could this be? The whole-word basals of that vintage provided extensive exposure—more than is done today—to the words introduced by repeating words within a book and in subsequent books.

I offer two related reasons for the misreading, both of which foreground the key role of learning letter–sound correspondences early in the acquisition of reading. First, the period in which I used the Dick and Jane materials was the heyday of the whole-word/look-say orientation in which the approach for teaching words was to memorize them. The pedagogical strategies involved presenting new words in sentences and in isolation, matching them to pictures, cutting up sentence strips and reading the words, putting the words back into sentences, and the like. It was my experience that early on—when the word corpus was small—these multiple exposures to whole words seemed to work for most children.

Here let me suggest that because whole-word procedures work when the word corpus is small, many children pay little, if any, attention to all the constituent parts of words. Moreover, the need for looking at all the letters in words is not particularly obvious. Observations of young children's first unguided attempts to use print show that they often find a distinctive feature as a cue to identify a word (Gough & Hillinger, 1980). Distinctive features might include a picture or a page location (e.g., *owl* is the last short string of letters on the page with a picture of birds), a mental image (e.g., *yellow* is a long string of letters with two straight lines in the middle), or initial letters, which are frequently used as recall cues (e.g., *birthday* starts with *b*).

Such word recognition involves "rote associations between unanalyzed spoken words and one or more salient and often arbitrary graphic feature of the printed word or its context" (Share, 1995, p. 159). Spelling-to-speech connections at subword units play little, if any, role. Thus, the whole-word/look-say method for teaching word recognition resembles the teaching of Chinese, a logographic-like writing system in which one symbol often represents an entire word. But it takes a very long time to learn to read Chinese, and it is not expected that students learn more than a few hundred items per year (Mason, Anderson, Omura, Uchida, & Imai, 1989; Perfetti & Zhang, 1996).

I believe that in the Dick and Jane materials, as the number of words grew, those children who hadn't induced spelling–sound relationships simply could not keep up. The arbitrary graphic features they may have been using as recall cues lost their power. In this regard, Share (1995) emphasizes a point noted by others (see, for example, Ehri, 1991; Perfetti, 1992), that "it is questionable whether providing the identity of a printed word at the whole-word level is likely to draw a child's attention to the detailed orthographic structure which ultimately forms the basis for proficient word recognition" (p. 153).

A second and intimately related issue that I think caused some of my first graders to be in big trouble at the end of first-grade concerns the vocabulary used in the early Dick and Jane materials. Specifically, the words included in the early text materials of the whole-word basals were selected on the basis of frequency in the language and the likelihood that young children would know those words from their aural repertoires. For example, stories could have included words such as *coat, boy, hot, cookies, no,* and *slow* in close proximity. Although all the words contain the letter *o,* the spelling-to-sound pattern is unique in each. When frequency is the major criteria for selecting words, the result is the inclusion of many complex spelling patterns as well as irregular words. Including many words in early texts that represent complex spelling-to-sound patterns makes it difficult to induce the systematicity of the print-to-speech mapping system. Thus, in terms of the kinds of words that children encounter in early texts, Juel and Roper-Schneider (1985) have noted that "the types of words which appear in beginning reading texts may well exert a more powerful influence in shaping children's word identification strategies than the method of reading instruction" (p. 151).

CONCLUSIONS AND MISUNDERSTANDINGS FROM TEACHING FIRST GRADE

Although I had some misgivings about how those 15 kind of shaky readers would fare, my general conclusion was optimistic. That is, if they didn't get discouraged, they'd be all right. It would just take them longer. I was, however, not sanguine about the remaining poor readers.

My optimistic conclusion was likely wrong for many children and perhaps dangerous for some. Current research now offers persuasive evidence that children who get off to a slow start rarely become strong readers (Stanovich, 1986). There are many reasons that this is the case. Early learning of the code leads to wider reading habits both in and out of school (Juel, 1988). Wide reading provides opportunities to grow in vocabulary, concepts, and knowledge of how text is written. Children who do not learn to decode do not have this avenue for growth. This phenomenon of the "rich get richer" (i.e., the children who learn early to decode continue to improve in their reading) and the "poor get poorer" (i.e., children who do not learn to decode early become increasingly distanced in reading ability from the "rich") has been termed the "Matthew effect" (Stanovich, 1986). A particularly chilling finding about the results of a weak start comes from Juel's (1988) longitudinal study of 54 children from first through fourth grade that showed a 0.88 probability that a child at the bottom quartile on the IOWA Reading Comprehension subtest at the end of first-grade would still be a poor reader at the end of fourth grade. A similar finding was identified earlier by Clay (1979).

Now I'd like to discuss the 15 or so children I described above as shaky. They read correctly, but they didn't seem to have confidence. I observed this even more clearly when I taught third grade. I would tell such kids, "You're right. You're doing fine. Have more confidence." It didn't help; they just weren't as confident as the good readers.

At a colloquium that Charles Perfetti gave in the 1970s, I became acquainted with issues of automaticity of lower-level processes and, as they say, the lightbulb went on. What I had mistaken for lack of confidence was more likely a lack of automaticity, producing an instructional implication different from the one I had developed.

Research over the last several decades has made it abundantly clear that comprehension, which of course is the purpose of reading, is not a single process; rather, it is a complex process made up of many interrelated component subprocesses (Just & Carpenter, 1987; Perfetti, 1985). The subprocesses include recognizing words and associating them with concepts stored in memory, developing meaningful ideas from strings of words (phrases, clauses, sentences), drawing inferences and relating what is already known to what is being read, and more. For a reader to comprehend a text, all these mental operations must take place, some of them concurrently. But it is well established that human information processing is limited (Kiss & Savage, 1977); that is, people simply cannot pay attention to too many things at once. Thus, when a complex process comprises a number of subprocesses, some of the lower-level processes must be developed so they can be carried out without direct attention, or automatically.

The negative impact of engaging in a complex process in which a lower-level subprocess has not been developed to automaticity is easily recognized in the psychomotor domain. For example, compare a competent basketball player and a novice basketball player as each dribbles during a game. The competent individual dribbles efficiently, giving no conscious attention to dribbling. That individual can direct attention to the higher-level components of the game, such as avoiding a steal, getting into position to pass, or maneuvering to a place where the ball can be dunked.

Now think of a youngster who knows how to dribble but needs to pay a certain amount of conscious attention to dribbling to do it well. In a game, if that child devotes too much attention to dribbling, the higher-level components such as passing and shooting may not be performed successfully. But if the novice diverts too much attention to the higher-level components, dribbling ability could break down, and he might lose the ball.

I consider word recognition somewhat analogous to dribbling. While one might argue the appropriateness of the analogy, the dependency of comprehension on efficient levels of word recognition processes is arguably not arguable. Adams & Bruck summarize the point as

> scientific research converges on the point that the association of spellings with sounds is a fundamental step in the early stages of literacy instruction. . . . There are literally hundreds of articles to support [this] conclusion. Over and over, children's knowledge of the correspondences between spellings and sounds is found to predict the speed and accuracy with which they can read single words, while the speed and accuracy with which they can read single words is found to predict their ability to comprehend written text. (1995, p. 15)

TEACHING ARMY SERGEANTS TO READ

After I finished my second year of first-grade teaching I went to Fort Smith, Arkansas, for personal reasons. There were no available jobs in the public schools, but through a serendipitous circumstance, I got a job at Camp Chaffee, an Army base, teaching non-commissioned officers (NCOs), mostly sergeants, to read. Some of the NCOs could read, albeit haltingly, and the Army had Reader's Digest *kinds of things for them. However, others virtually could not read at all. What to do with those?*

Not to worry! The Army had figured it all out. It had developed a basal directly modeled on the Dick and Jane materials. The first page introduced a young man in a farm scene. On the next two pages were his mother in her apron canning something and his father on a tractor waving to a neighbor. Turn the page, and there's a recruiting sergeant! In contrast to Dick and Jane, who visit the country, Pete joins the Army to serve his country. And instead of sentences like "Dick and Jane ride in the car. They are riding to grandfather's,", the Army basal said, "Pete rides the bus. He is riding to the Army camp."

I knew exactly how to teach that kind of basal with its whole-word, look-say approach, and I worked very hard to do it well. I introduced new words in context sentences; we practiced reading the sentences; we reviewed the words on flashcards; we read the story silently, then orally, and so on. And it didn't work—not even a little. The men forgot words virtually immediately. In frustration, I began to break rules I had learned about teaching beginning reading. I found myself saying things like "Look, it says bus. bbuuss. *Sergeant Hiram, point to the letters in* bbuuss *and say the sounds slowly." It seemed that with that kind of showing and practicing, I could see a crack here and there in the bleakness of these men's memory for words.*

What was I doing? Well, I was teaching phonics, and I was making it up along the way. Phonics had been mentioned in the one reading methods class I had taken, but it had seemed to me to have a negative connotation. And the "phonetic" [sic] analysis in the Dick and Jane manuals I had been using in my first-grades didn't get much beyond initial and, maybe, final consonant sounds. It was easy to see that it was often the sequence of letters after the initial one that caused my sergeants the most trouble. When they got to a word in text that they didn't recognize, some of the men would start it correctly, but after the initial sound they'd switch to a word that made sense in the context, even when it didn't begin with the initial sound of the target word (not unlike some of my first graders). With the sergeants, however, I started to insist that they stay with the correct beginning sound and try to figure out the word. (I had not done that with my first graders, because I had learned in college and from the Dick and Jane manuals just to tell them the words they couldn't read, so as not to interrupt meaning.) Moreover, perhaps I "saw" what the sergeants were doing because, in contrast to 40-some children, many of whom did not have problems reading, I worked with small classes, often on a one-to-one basis.

So, as noted, during the time I was with the sergeants, I began to insist that they try to figure out a word after they produced an initial correct sound. At first, chaos broke out: bus *might become* bat; truck *might become* take, *and the like. They didn't like that because they knew it didn't make sense. They would have much preferred to read* truck *as* vehicle, *but I wouldn't let them because doing so would not have advanced them on the road to independent reading. What I did do was require that they deal with the sounds of every letter from the beginning to the end of a word. (In retrospect, the idea was right, but my procedures were primitive.) Be that as it may, what I was doing began to work a little, and some of the virtually nonreading sergeants began to pick their way through "Private Pete in Basic Training" texts, menus, and movie marquees. The men and I were very happy.*

Enormously important to the development of my understanding of how to teach these men was that when I asked, they would tell me what I did that helped. Most often the things that helped had something to do with showing them how the system between print and speech connects—although those were not their words or, for that matter, mine.

After several years with these men, my conclusion was that the reason they needed such explicit instruction was that when they first went to school they were probably not "ready" to learn to read. And some of not being ready could be attributed to their coming from backgrounds with very limited exposure to print.

Before providing an analysis of my conclusion about the men in Arkansas, I turn to what I learned about beginning reading from my two children, Mark and Elizabeth.

OBSERVING MY OWN CHILDREN'S LITERACY DEVELOPMENT

When my children were growing up, our home was print rich, language rich, and child centered. Let me give you a glimpse of both of them as they engaged in one aspect of literacy. I'll start with Mark, who, at age 5, moved some magnetic letters on the re-frigerator around and formed the sequence t i i p, *asked me to try to figure out what it said but warned me that although it was a real word, it wasn't spelled right. I read* type *and* tip. *"No. No." And with lots of giggling Mark told me that there was a clue in the word* portion *that was in a recipe on the refrigerator. When that didn't help me, Mark told me that the word was* ship. *I didn't get it and asked how* portion *should have helped me figure out that* t i i p *was* ship. *With that Mark pointed to the* t i *in* portion *and said, "See."*

Now let me tell you about Elizabeth. She adored books, she begged to be read to, and her father and I were enormously responsive. Elizabeth did not engage with the magnetic letters on the refrigerator. Instead, she drew pictures of stories we read to her for magnetic posting on the refrigerator, and she dictated notes to the characters. Elizabeth wasn't interested in letters or words; she was interested in stories and ideas and feelings.

Let me compare what happened to Mark and Elizabeth in school. Both went to the same kind of first grade, one with the whole-word approach to reading. Mark flourished as a reader, but, Mark would have flourished in any context. Without having been directly taught, Mark's figuring out the print-to-speech system was quite extraordinary. Elizabeth did not flourish, and the print-rich environment in which she grew up did not help her to notice the patterns in written language.

Elizabeth's teacher told me not to worry. She was so creative and smart that she was sure to catch on. I believed as her teacher did. But Elizabeth knew she wasn't doing well and eventually showed her unhappiness, at which point I set about to teach her. And what did I teach her? I taught her what I taught my sergeants. I taught her the letter/sound mappings directly and systematically. But I did it less primitively, albeit not optimally.

Anyway, Elizabeth learned what she was taught, but she had to be taught everything. Somehow, despite growing up in a print-rich environment with sympathetic and encouraging parents, Elizabeth did not figure out many of the intricacies required to apply the alphabetic principle.

As an aside, for those of you who have your own Elizabeths, I can report that she is an excellent and avid reader. You know, as Elizabeth grew up she articulated her learning-to-read experiences, and there was a period in her life when she would tell me often that she knew she had been lucky to have me. And she was. But 15 of my first graders (and maybe as many as 30) were not lucky to have me.

ANALYSIS OF WHAT I LEARNED ABOUT READING FROM MY OWN CHILDREN

My children's stories point to two important issues. First, the Elizabeth story renders at least partly suspect my conclusion that the reason my sergeants needed to have the code systematically presented was that they had not come from print-rich backgrounds. Leaving the acquisition of reading aside for a moment, the face validity of the advantages of a literacy-rich home in which parents often read to and talk with their children about what they read cannot and, in my opinion, must not be denied. Among the advantages are learning about the wonders that can be encountered between the covers of books, including both knowledge about the world and the universality of human feelings. So, who would not wish that all children could have the thousands of hours of literacy experiences that Elizabeth had? But all that experience did not make early reading acquisition easy for Elizabeth. Is she rare? No.

One of the important lessons my children's stories point to is that of individual differences. It seems clear that individual differences account for the enormous dissimilarity in Mark and Elizabeth's early competence with words and subword units. In this regard, Share and Stanovich (1995) have described the problems of Elizabeth and her counterparts (e.g., some of my first graders and sergeants) as follows:

> Successful reading acquisition seems to require the development of an analytic processing stance towards words that is probably not the "natural" processing set adopted by most children and some children have extreme difficulty in adopting an analytic processing set. The latter group will, as a result, have considerable difficulty building up knowledge of subword spelling–sound correspondences— and such knowledge appears to be a necessary prerequisite of fluent reading. (p. 153)

Relatedly, it should be noted that theories and research on individual differences point to inadequacies in converting spellings to sounds as the primary area that differentiates skilled from less skilled young readers (Stanovich, 1986). This finding is supported by current cognitive neuroscience findings (Shaywitz et al., 2003, 2004).

Finally, the gist of this prologue is: from the multiple lenses of having taught first graders and sergeants to read; from being familiar with large bodies of research about the psychology of word recognition and the role of lower-level processes in comprehension; from engaging in my own lines of related research; from watching my two children; from working with teachers training to become reading specialists; and from visits to current primary classrooms, I learned that children must gain control of the print-to-speech mapping system *early* if they are to become successful readers.

1

INTRODUCTION

The Prologue explains how I came to understand the critical importance of teaching the print-to-speech mapping system, or how letters represent specific sounds in words. After my work with the sergeants and during my work with Elizabeth, I began to develop specific approaches to help me teach the letter–sound system in efficient ways. Eventually, Rebecca Hamilton and I crafted a workshop about these approaches, which we presented for the American Federation of Teachers (AFT) at their Educational Research and Dissemination Institute in Baltimore (1996). Subsequently, written material was developed to go along with the workshop.

Although the written material provides detailed descriptions of procedures, it was not created for the purpose of conveying the underlying principles influencing their development. Thus, as I discovered the informal migration of the material—in large part by the AFT, as well as local school district administrators and my graduate students—I began to be concerned about the implementation of the approaches as merely recipes. The problem was that written explanations and rationales for the procedures were not provided; albeit when I presented them to students and at workshops, I did discuss the background and rationales. I became uneasy that the procedures were not being understood within a larger context that would explain the theoretical rationale for their use.

So in this book, I not only describe the instructional procedures, but also the explanations for their use. I have done this in two ways. One is the more conventional way of providing the theoretical basis and then offering examples. The second way is to provide examples and then explain them. It has been my experience that teachers appreciate examples. So, in many places in this book, I provide examples and then comment on them in terms of how and why they function. In this way, I hope that this book will go far beyond providing some useful ways for teachers to work on teaching word-level knowledge and skills to children. Rather, it is my hope that the analyses and commentary on the examples will provide and enhance theoretical understanding as well.

HOW THIS BOOK IS ORGANIZED

There are two main sections to this book: six chapters and six appendices. The chapters start with a discussion of issues about learning to read words and then move to presenting instructional procedures. Each procedure is analyzed through commentaries and discussion. The appendices provide materials to which the procedures can be applied.

There is this introductory chapter, then the second chapter deals with the alphabetic principle and phonics and considers what children need to know and be able to do to read words. It includes a discussion of terms that are used throughout the book. The third chapter is devoted to teaching letter–sound correspondences. The principles that underlie the instruction are discussed, including the role of phonemic awareness. Most of the chapter is devoted to presenting the instructional procedures and analyzing and commenting on their purpose and function. The fourth chapter considers issues in teaching children to blend letter–sounds into words. Why the blending process can be difficult and how that difficulty can be addressed are discussed. The fifth chapter introduces Word Building, an activity that supports decoding and word recognition by having children use letter cards to build words and then changing letters to build different words. These opportunities allow children consistently to experience and discriminate the effects on a word of changing one letter. The sixth chapter is devoted to multisyllabic words. I use the epilogue to make comments about several issues related to the teaching of reading.

WHAT THIS BOOK IS NOT
AND WHOM IT IS FOR

In describing what this book is, I start by ignoring a suggestion I make to my students: never begin a discussion of what something is by saying what it isn't.

Nevertheless, this book is *not* a reading curriculum. It is *not* a core reading program. Reading curricula and core reading programs need to be comprehensive, especially in terms of the inclusion of many stories and other text materials for children to read. What this book provides is a set of strategies and detailed procedures and accompanying material that encompass explicit, systematic phonics instruction. The strategies would be useful in programs that do not include explicit phonics. They can also be used to support and strengthen instructional procedures within current reading programs that do include phonics. The strategies can be used for immediate intervention or remedial instruction.

EXPLANATIONS OF TERMS

This section provides an explanation of terms used throughout the book. The terms are often confused or misunderstood, so I thought that having this resource up front would be helpful.

When individuals are **decoding** they are using the letters on a page to retrieve the sounds associated with those letters; that is, they see the letters *b, a,* and *t* in the word *bat,* and say /bat/. The retrieval may be instantaneous (the reader sees *bat* and reads /bat/), or it may be deliberate (the reader sees *Pugashefsky* and figures out its pronunciation, perhaps something like /puga/ /pug/ /a/ /shef/ /sky/). The difference between reading *bat* with no hesitation and perhaps faltering a moment on *Pugashefsky* is the difference in attention that the reader needs to pay to each word. At one end of the decoding process, readers apply letter–sound knowledge immediately, without any apparent attention. Common terms used to describe the immediate phenomenon are **word recognition** and **sight word recognition.** Another term associated with immediate word recognition is **automaticity.** Automaticity is used to indicate that a reader recognizes words virtually instantly, that is, without obvious overt attention.

At the other end of decoding, readers consciously and deliberately apply letter–sound knowledge to produce a plausible pronunciation of a word they do not recognize instantly. Children just learning to read will likely apply their knowledge deliberately, but adult readers may need to be deliberate when trying to pronounce a Russian name, a pharmacological term, or the like. The term associated with this self-aware figuring out is **word attack.** All the terms noted above fall under **decoding,** albeit decoding with different levels of conscious attention.

Encoding, often thought about as spelling, is the opposite of decoding. Here, an individual applies knowledge of letter–sound relationships to identify the letters that will be needed to make a specific written word. For instance, when you ask a person, "How do you spell *benign*?", you probably want to know the letters that make up the word so that you can write it.

English, like many other languages, is based on the **alphabetic principle.** That principle is that written words are composed of letters, and those letters correspond to segments of spoken words. In an alphabetic language, a letter, or **grapheme,** is associated with a unit of speech, or **phoneme.** For example, the grapheme *m* in the word *mop* is associated with the phoneme /m/. In contrast, in logographic languages, such as Chinese, one character can represent an entire word. Thus, reading Chinese does not depend on the alphabetic principle but on memorization of characters.

At a general level, **phonics** is the relationship between speech and print. It is also used as an umbrella term for various instructional strategies that are used to teach the relationships between print and speech.

The **Great Debate** is a term coined by Jeanne Chall in 1967 to describe a long-lasting argument in the reading field as to whether it is more useful to teach beginning readers a code-oriented approach or a meaning-oriented approach. More recently, code-oriented approaches are associated with phonics and meaning-oriented approach with whole-language and literature-based in-struction.

Explicit, systematic phonics refers to instructional strategies for teaching phonics. The explicit part means that the relationship between letters and sounds is directly pointed out. The systematic part refers to presenting those relationships in a pre-established sequence. There can be variations in the sequence. The first four letters of one reading program are *a, m, t, s*; the first four letters of another program are *a, r, t, n*. In most sequences, the consonants and short vowels are presented before long vowels and vowel digraphs are intro-duced.

Orthography is a language's writing (spelling) system, and **orthographic knowledge** is what an individual knows about a language's writing system. For example, young children have been known to write *CU* for *see you*, *bak* for *back*, and *bot* for *boat*. Such examples of what has been called "invented spelling" are children's attempts to represent their oral language in written language. Even-tually children's orthographic knowledge will grow, and they will be able to rep-resent their oral language through the conventions of English orthography.

The **consonant** letters in English are *b, c, d, f, g, h, j, k, l, m, n, p, q, r, s, t, v, w, x, y,* and *z*. **Consonant blends,** sometimes called **consonant clusters,** are two or three contiguous consonant letters. For example, the letters *br* in *brush* are a consonant blend, as are the letters *spl* in *split*. Each of the consonants in a consonant blend maintains its sound. That is, if you say *split,* you will utter the phonemes for *s* and *p* and *l*. In contrast, in **consonant digraphs,** such as the *sh* in *ship* and the *th* in *thin,* the individual letters do not maintain their phonemes. That is, when one says *ship,* the *s* phoneme as in *sat* and the *h* phoneme, as in *him,* are not produced; rather, the two letters *sh* represent a unique sound.

The **vowel** letters in English are *a, e, i, o, and u*. Sometimes *y* acts as a vowel, such as in *try*. When instructional materials talk about **short vowels,** they most often are referring to *a* as in *mat, e* as in *ten, i* as in *pin, o* as in *hot,* and *u* as in *hut*. Most **long vowels** fall into three major groups. One is the CVC*e* (consonant–vowel–consonant–*e*) in which the final *e* is silent and the first vowel represents a long sound. *Kite, make,* and *bone* are examples of CVC*e* words. Additionally, there are several vowel combinations, especially **vowel digraphs** and **vowel diphthongs**. Vowel digraphs are long vowel sounds represented by two adjacent letters. For example, the words *seat, rain, teeth,* and *play* have the vowel digraphs *ea, ai, ee,* and *ay*. A **diphthong** is a single speech sound that begins with one vowel sound and moves to another, as in the words *cow, few,* and *soil*. Children do not need to know the distinction between vowel digraphs and vowel diphthongs. (Did you, before you read this?) Instruction merely needs to be focused on the vowel sound in a word that is represented by two adjacent letters. In English, the letter *r* often influences how a preceding vowel is pronounced. Vowels followed by *r* are known as *r*-**controlled vowels**. Notice the differences in pronunciation between the following word pairs: *cat, car; sit, sir.*

A **phoneme** is the smallest speech sound into which a spoken word can be divided. The word *mat* has three phonemes, *jump* has four phonemes, and *chain* has three phonemes (/ch/ /ai/ /n/). Conventionally, phonemes are presented in writing between two slash marks // and in the International Phonetic Alphabet (IPA) notation. In this book, the IPA notation will not be used because learning the notation requires study time. Instead, phonemes will be presented through normal letters within slashes //. So, the sound associated the letter *f* will be represented as /f/ and the long-vowel combination *ai* as /ai/.

A **grapheme** is the smallest written representation of speech sounds: *man* has three graphemes (*m, a, n*), *jump* has four graphemes (*j, u, m, p*), and *chain* has three graphemes (*ch, ai, n*).

Grapheme–phoneme correspondences and **letter–sound correspondences** are expressions used to label the correspondence between a grapheme and a phoneme (e.g., the grapheme–phoneme relationships in *dip* are *d* /d/, *i* /i/, *p* /p/).

The expression **spelling–sound relationships** encompasses the notion that readers are able to use various subword units often beyond grapheme–phoneme relationship when decoding (e.g., *ous, an, tion*).

Phonological awareness is an umbrella term for an individual's understanding of spoken words, including being able to identify words that rhyme, a word that is different in a set of words, and words that begin or end with the same sound. **Phonemic awareness** is an individual's understanding of the individual phonemes in a word (e.g., that *ran* and *rain* both have three phonemes). The meanings of these terms will become clearer as you encounter them in the context of the explanations provided in the chapters that follow.

2

THE ALPHABETIC PRINCIPLE AND PHONICS

Lisa, a student in a master's-level university reading course, had been anxiously telling me about Theresa, a child in her second grade with "strange" word recognition problems. "Strange" because she could read a lot of words that were "harder" than those she missed. Lisa was particularly concerned that, in the middle of Theresa's second-grade year, the percentage of words she read incorrectly seemed to be increasing. Lisa brought in the results of Theresa's performance on some word-recognition tests so we could examine the problem. Below are selected words from several word-recognition lists that Lisa had administered to Theresa. The words in **bold** are those that Theresa did not attempt as well as those that she read incorrectly.

an	he
and	here
are	hot
bat	**me**
be	men
boy	off
but	on
can	tree
cut	with
down	work
go	yellow

19

Examination of some of the words Theresa got wrong and some of the words she read correctly provide a hint about Theresa's problem. The hint is hard to detect in the format in which the words are presented above. See if the hint is more available in the presentation of some further selected words below. Again, the words Theresa read incorrectly are in **bold**.

an
and
bat
but
cut
he
hot
me
mom
no
not

As one more presentation of Theresa's problem, some of the words that Theresa read correctly are in the first column and words that she read incorrectly are in the second column.

Words known	Words not known
and	an
bat	but
cut	me
he	not
hot	
mom	
no	

Notice that Theresa could read *and*, but she could not delete the *d* and read *an*. She was able to read *bat* and *cut*, but she apparently was not able to use the *b* and *t* in *bat* and the *u* (or the *ut*) in *cut* to read *but*. Theresa could read *mom* and *he*, but couldn't use the appropriate phonemes from those words to read *me*. Finally, she was unable to read *not*, even though she was able to read *hot* and *no*.

Theresa is a quintessential example of a child who has virtually no understanding of the alphabetic principle. That principle is that the sounds within spoken words are represented in writing by letters, and that those letters represent the sounds rather consistently.

Although Theresa's instructional experiences had included only superficial phonics, a question of interest is how a bright child (and Theresa was bright) could still not have figured out the alphabetic principle. Many of her classmates had, even though, like Theresa, they were not directly taught to do so. Why not Theresa? The answer is that some people just don't—remember Elizabeth. Some interesting evidence associated with the "some folks just don't" notion comes from the work of Bishop (1964) who simulated the beginning reading experience by teaching college students to read some Arabic words. The eight Arabic words used in the experiment contained twelve letters for which there were perfect letter–sound correspondences.

In the Bishop study, there were two experimental groups. One group was taught a set of words, all of which were composed of the twelve letters, through a whole-word approach (seeing and hearing a word until it is remembered). The other group was taught the letter–sound correspondences of the twelve letters. The groups were then compared on their ability to read a set of transfer words (i.e., words that were not used in instruction, but that contained the letter–sound correspondences that had been taught and used in instructional words). The results of a transfer test showed that the letter–sound group performed best. But 12 of the 20 members of the whole-word group obtained scores similar to those of the letter–sound group. When asked how they read the words, some members of the word group reported that they had tried to figure out the letter–sounds within the words and thus had extrapolated the letter–sound correspondences from the training words. As such, these adults used the alphabetic principle. This is far from surprising given that they were college students who read English well. What is of great interest is that 8 of the 20 adult participants in the word group did not attempt to use the alphabetic principle, even though they were fully aware of it, and instead apparently attempted to memorize the words. Thus, it should not be too surprising that some 7-year-olds will not figure out the alphabetic principle on their own.

So what do we do about Theresa? Lisa believed that Theresa needed drill on the words that she did not read correctly. It interested me that Lisa's suggestion of what to do about the child's problem reminded me how much I would have agreed with her in the earlier days of my public school teaching career. In fact, flashcard drill was, as I mentioned in the prologue, exactly what I did with my first graders who were having difficulty. But, both Lisa and I were wrong! Theresa's large sight vocabulary had masked her lack of phonics knowledge.

A misleading phenomenon for both Lisa and the earlier me is that repeated word drills can produce a result. In fact, I would guess that if Lisa had done flashcard drills on the words that Theresa had not read correctly in the examples above and other words that Theresa didn't know, there would have been improvement on those words. That is, with her apparently good visual memory, Theresa probably would have learned some more sight words. But Theresa would have "hit the wall" sooner or later because of her astonishing lack of understanding of the alphabetic principle. What Theresa clearly needed was phonics.

Lisa did provide Theresa with some phonics. She taught Theresa some letter–sound correspondences and how to blend those sounds. Actually Lisa used procedures similar to the ones provided in this book—although not as complete—for letter–sound and blending instruction. But Lisa's initiation of phonics with Theresa did not go easily at first. Theresa objected to the procedures. In fact, she actually asked Lisa to teach her the words she didn't know, but not to do it with the sounds. Figuring out words through their sounds slowed Theresa down and was not satisfying. She just wanted to read the words. Notice how much the comment by Share and Stanovich (1995) that I noted earlier captures Lisa's experience with Theresa:

> An analytic processing stance towards words . . . is probably not the "natural" processing set adopted by most children and some children have extreme difficulty in adopting an analytic processing set. The latter group will, as a result, have considerable difficulty building up knowledge of subword spelling—sound correspondences. (p. 153)

But Lisa persisted with some motivational devices, and eventually Theresa loved decoding words she hadn't been able to read, and her reading took off. My point in telling the story is not to show what phonics can do, but rather to indicate that if a teacher knows why she is doing something—in conversations with me and readings that I provided in the course, Lisa came to understand Theresa's problems at a deep level—she can have confidence in what she is doing, in spite of some less than smooth lessons.

As mentioned, Theresa's large sight vocabulary had masked her lack of phonics knowledge, and it took some digging to uncover her problem. The next example presents a more obvious diagnosis. To begin, look at the results of a pseudoword test given to a first grader in March who was not making progress in reading. The teacher knew he had decoding problems, but didn't know the extent of it because she thought that some of his lack of phonics knowledge might be masked by some sight word knowledge. The extent of this first-grade child's decoding problem is captured vividly by the results of the pseudoword assessment below.

Pseudoword	Child's response
kot	ka
swip	s
gan	ga
dree	da . . . er
shub	ser
doy	ba
cho	ka . . . we
flate	fa
meep	mech
dut	da . . . u
pog	pa . . . u . . . ch
nack	na
fet	fee
han	ere

The results suggest that the child had some knowledge of the first sound in a syllable but was virtually unable to decode the vowel and final phoneme. The called-for remediation was teaching vowel sounds and how to blend all the sounds into a word.

There is some controversy associated with testing decoding through pseudowords. Some say that asking children to decode print to speech when the resultant utterance will not be a word they know is a poor measure of reading and should not be taken as a measure of competence. Presently, however, many in the field would indicate that the use of pseudowords for assessment can be very informative.

In the case of the first-grade child under consideration, it would likely have been difficult to see what phonic elements the child needed to learn without the pseudoword test. This story had at least a short-term positive outcome. That is, through three months of special small-group instruction, with emphasis on vowels, blending, and Word Building, the child's pseudoword results, as well as normal reading, improved dramatically. I do not know what happened later, but it seemed that he had made an important inroad: he understood the alphabetic principle and some of the details of it. Of course, that is not enough, and this child, whom I did meet, will probably need extra support, but at least at the end of first grade, he was in the reading ballpark.

■ YOUR TURN ■

Consider the following responses on a word-recognition test taken by a third grader.

Word	Student read
cold	could
soon	same
war	wear
figure	finger
certain	curtur
mineral	material
paragraph	potograph
describe	decided
century	country

Carefully examine the child's responses to each of the target words. Analyze what you think he is doing with each word. For example, the child's reading of *could* for *cold* suggests that he paid attention to the beginning and final grapheme, ignored the middle, and pulled from his repertoire a word he's seen often. Keep your analysis of this third grader's responses and return to it when you finish the book.

WHAT IS PHONICS?

Recently, I was in a line at the post office and overheard two mothers in conversation. I moved to full-fledged eavesdropping when I recognized that the conversation was about their 6-year-old boys and how they were learning to read in different schools. Early in the conversation, one of the mothers asked the other whether her child was learning phonics, and the other asked what she meant. Both of these young women were clearly intelligent and educated, so it may surprise those of you who are reading this book that some people don't know what phonics is.

As it turned out, the first mother's reply to the second mother was right on: "It's [phonics] about the relationship between letters and their sounds." That, indeed, is what phonics is, and nobody has ever argued that knowing phonics is not important. At the extreme, the Great Debate was about whether phonics should be taught directly or whether it should be brought to children's attention indirectly and derived from whole-word knowledge. With the Reading First Initiative (Armbruster, Lehr, & Osborn, 2001) by the federal government, "explicit, systematic phonics" has come to the fore. Note that this is profoundly different from the commercial whole-word programs of a quarter of a century ago as well as the commercial literature-based programs of a decade ago. I, for one, believe from the field's data and my own experiences that explicit, systematic phonics holds the advantage. The influence of Reading First on the major commercial reading programs has been profound. To the best of my knowledge, all basal programs in their current editions have provided explicit, systematic phonics instruction, although there is likely variation in the quality of that instruction.

WHAT DO CHILDREN NEED TO KNOW AND BE ABLE TO DO TO READ WORDS?

- They need to know the speech sounds associated with written letters in words.
- They need to know how to put those sounds together to form a pronounceable word.
- They need to have a strong sense of English orthography.
- They need to recognize words rapidly.

I will deal with each of those components in the chapters that follow. But for now, it may help set the backdrop for this book if you would reflect a few moments about some of the students in your class.

■ YOUR TURN ■

Make a list of several of your best readers and several of your weakest readers. Turn each of the four statements above into a question (e.g., "Does this student know the sounds represented by the letter and letter combinations in the words he should be reading?")

Rate each student as high, medium, or low for the four questions. Note that the four questions can be asked at first grade and higher grades, as the four components are needed at all grade levels, albeit for increasingly complex words.

Look at the results and determine the extent to which there is a different profile for the strong and weak readers. You may want to keep these students in mind as the instructional strategies in this book are presented.

3

LETTER–SOUND INSTRUCTION

In this chapter, I build on the concepts of the alphabetic principle and phonics provided in Chapter 2. I describe how to introduce children to the letter–sound relationships for consonants, vowels, and sounds represented by more than one letter, such as the long *e* vowel sound spelled *ea*.

Let's start with the purpose of teaching phonics, which is to be able to decode words. Given this purpose, it follows that very early in the instructional sequence children should experience decoding some words. It's like when children take piano lessons and learn to play little pieces when they can read only a few notes. By playing the piece, they experience what those few notes can do. Similarly, in the early phases of learning to read, children should be provided with the knowledge and skills that enable them actually to decode some words.

Although the idea of decoding simple words early on seems an obvious goal for children who are learning to read, traditional practices have not made this possible. As seasoned teachers recall, not too long ago many commercial reading programs and reading education textbooks recommended teaching children most of the consonant sounds before introducing vowels. Furthermore, the emphasis was on teaching the consonants only in the initial position. I continue to encounter teachers of young children who believe that teaching most consonants in initial position and then vowels is the way to go. The "consonants-before-vowels" notion is likely based on the fact that there is mostly a one-to-one relationship between consonant letters and the sounds they represent: *b* is always /b/, *j* is always /j/. But there is not a one-to-one relationship between vowel letters and the sounds they represent. *A* can represent the short sound as in *can,* or *a* can be *r*-controlled as in *car,* or *a* can be part of a vowel digraph as in *rain.* Certainly it would not be wise to teach the complexities of vowels early. But some simple vowel–sound relationships can be taught early. And the reason, of course, is that a vowel is needed in order to produce any English word. Without knowledge of the sound of a vowel, the experience of figuring out the pronunciation of a word is not possible.

PRINCIPLES FOR TEACHING LETTER–SOUND CORRESPONDENCES

Two major principles underlie the instructional strategies for teaching the letter–sound correspondences that follow. One is that early in the instructional sequence for teaching a letter–sound relationship (e.g., the written *b* represents the /b/ in spoken words) attention is brought to the target in all positions in which it is found in a word. Simply put, children need to learn that a *b* is /b/ in *bat* as well as in *cab,* and they need to learn this from the beginning of *b* to /b/ instruction.

There is evidence that most children, even those who have empirically demonstrable inadequate decoding skills, are able to decode the first letter, or grapheme, in a word (McCandliss, Beck, Sandak, & Perfetti, 2003). But poor readers do not decode the last graphemes in words well, and they are especially poor at decoding the medial grapheme (McCandliss et al., 2003).

The study by McCandliss and others described an intervention with children who had inadequate decoding skills after 1–3 years of schooling. A pretest showed that they could correctly decode the first grapheme in a word 70% of the time, the final grapheme 54%, and the medial, which was a vowel, 40% of the time. It is likely that it is both the within-word position and the vowel on its own that causes the medial decoding problem. But whatever the cause, given the role of vowels in English, the results above suggest that, at best, the children could read merely 40% of the pretest words. Needless to say, this is enormously serious for children's progress as readers.

Certainly the nature of the vowel is part of the problem. Depending on the letter environment in which a vowel grapheme is found, there are several possible phonemes or pronunciations. In single syllable words, vowels are often found in the medial position, and so the medial position is likely a difficulty factor in decoding, too. The notion that letter position plays a role in the decoding problems is supported by the McCandliss (2003) data. Note, as mentioned above, children could decode the final grapheme less well than the initial grapheme. And in the single-syllable words used in the McCandliss study, the final grapheme was not a vowel.

The second principle for the letter–sound instructional strategies that follow is that phoneme awareness is specifically folded into the teaching of letter–sound correspondences. This contrasts with typical phonemic awareness instruction, which deals with sounds in spoken words with no letters present—a speech-related activity practiced in the absence of print. There are several implications for instruction of the second principle. The major one is that sophisticated phonemic awareness (e.g., say the sounds in *noise*; say *track* without the /r/) is not a prerequisite for learning letter–sound correspondences. That is, children do not need to be able to identify from a spoken word all the sounds in that word or be able to remove a sound from a spoken word to make a new word before they learn that *t* represents /t/.

PERSPECTIVES ON THE ROLE OF PHONEMIC AWARENESS

It is important to note that there are studies that support the use of phonemic awareness as a speech-related practice in the absence of print (Bentin & Leshem, 1993; Hurford, Schauf, Bunce, Blaich, & Moore, 1994). However, an emerging consensus suggests that, beyond preschool, phonemic awareness instruction is most effective when such instruction is imparted in the context of printed letters. (See National Reading Panel, 2000, and Bus & van IJzendoorn, 1999, for two recent meta-analyses.)

There are three perspectives relevant to the role of phonemic awareness. One is that phonemic awareness is a prerequisite to learning to decode (Liberman & Shankweiler, 1979). A strict prerequisite position would assume that children must have a degree of phonemic awareness prior to learning about decoding. The idea is that decoding instruction will move along better if children start it with phonemic awareness capability. Another perspective is that phonemic awareness is a byproduct of learning to decode (e.g., Morais, Cary,

Alegria, & Bertleson, 1979). From this perspective, simply learning to decode will result in phonemic awareness even though no phonemic awareness is explicitly taught. In the Morais and others (1979) work, adult illiterates who did not have phonemic awareness gained it when taught to read.

I was intrigued by the finding from this study because I think I sensed something similar when I taught the Army sergeants. In those days, I had not heard of phonemic awareness, and I don't think it was only because I was young and inexperienced. I just don't think the notions were present in the field. Anyway, as I noted earlier, I eventually had some success in teaching my sergeants some phonics, and they did learn how to figure out the pronunciations of not too complex words by producing the sounds, or phonemes, represented by the letters. My sense that these men were acquiring phonemic awareness came from incidents such as a man who finally decoded *tent,* looking up and saying something like, "Oh yeah, *tent* has four sounds." Another man noticed that *tents* had "one more sound than *tent.*" Certainly such distant and anecdotal evidence is at best merely a vague impression, but that impression came to mind when I read about the Morais work.

The third perspective about the nature of the relationship between phonemic awareness and decoding (the reciprocal perspective) captures elements of both the prerequisite position and the byproduct position. According to the reciprocal perspective, instructional activities focused on teaching decoding will lead to gains in phonemic awareness, and additional activities directed at analysis of only spoken words may not be necessary. The most complex forms of phonemic awareness—those that require manipulation of speech segments such as elision in spoken pseudowords (e.g., say *splend* without the /p/)—are promoted by learning to decode. For example, children can gain the ability to engage in elision tasks on written language (e.g., remove the /r/ in the written *track,* and read the resultant word). Such integration with written language should enhance speech-only phonemic awareness (e.g., say *track* without the /r/).

Here, I need to share a concern that in the instructional domain, phonemic awareness may be taking on more of a life of its own than is useful. For example, I know of several second-grade teachers who have children who are not decoding well having asked for help from their reading coaches to provide phonemic awareness instruction to those children, even though the children can successfully engage in relatively easy phonemic awareness tasks as oral blending and identifying words that begin with the same sounds. With the skills they have, these children have enough phonemic awareness competency to support decoding instruction, and the appropriate instructional recommendation is that they receive more intense decoding rather than phonemic awareness instruction. There is no evidence that trying to improve reading by asking such children to engage in sophisticated speech-only tasks (e.g., say *splash* without the /p/) will improve decoding. In fact, think of how much your knowledge of English orthography is what enables you to say *splash* without the /p/.

Both time and effectiveness should be considered here. The time issue is about delaying reading instruction in order to engage children in sophisticated phonemic awareness training. The effectiveness issue is about the impact of advanced phonemic awareness training on children's reading success. I address both issues by presenting instructional strategies that require only a small degree of phonemic awareness, while integrating phonemic awareness into the instruction. In this way, children can begin learning about letter–sounds and reading words while learning that spoken words comprise several sounds.

TEACHING LETTER–SOUND RELATIONSHIPS

Before presenting lessons for introducing letter–sound relationships, I want to point out that I have made use of a "script" format. That is, I have provided the actual words or dialogue that a teacher might use in teaching the lessons. I did this because it is an economical way of presenting the information, not because I expect teachers to use the exact words that I have chosen. My intention is not just to provide the steps in a procedure, but also to share the reasons for the steps. As teachers become familiar with the procedures and principles underlying their use, they can then adapt the dialogue to meet the needs of their students and to reflect their own teaching style.

MATERIALS

To teach the lessons for letter–sound relationships represented by consonants, you will need the following materials.

- Large letter cards that you can use for demonstration purposes
- Pocket chart for displaying the large letter cards

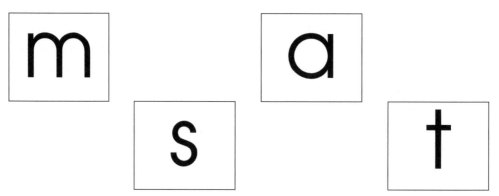

- A set of individual letter cards for each student
- Individual Word Pockets for each student to use in sorting and displaying letters

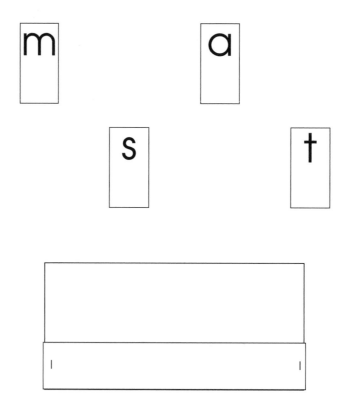

The letter cards and directions for making the Word Pocket can be found in Appendix F.

LESSON SEQUENCE FOR TEACHING CONSONANT LETTER–SOUND CORRESPONDENCE

The goal of the lessons that follow is for a child to be able to look at letters in words and say the speech sounds that those letters represent. The six steps in the lesson for teaching a consonant letter–sound correspondence are as follows:

1. Develop phonemic awareness by focusing children's attention on the sound represented by a particular letter in the initial position.
2. Connect the printed letter with the sound the letter represents.
3. Discriminate among words that have the letter–sound in the initial position and those that do not.
4. Develop phonemic awareness by focusing children's attention on the sound represented by a particular letter in the final position.
5. Discriminate among words that have the letter–sound in the final position and those that do not.
6. Discriminate among words that have the letter–sound in the initial and final positions.

In the sample lesson that follows, you can see how the sequence is carried out.

A Sample Lesson for Teaching the Letter–Sound Correspondence for *m* /m/

On pages 34–37, using the *m* as an example, the steps for teaching consonant letter–sound correspondences are given in detail. Many steps are followed by a commentary explaining why the step is provided and how it might function in children's learning.

Focus of lesson sequence	Procedure
1. Develop phonemic awareness of the target sound in the initial position.	*I know a story with a character called Mary Mouse who drank lots of milk.* Who drank the milk? The words Mary *and* Mouse *begin with the same sound: the /m/ sound.* Watch my mouth: /m/. You say /m/.

Commentary: The purpose of this phonemic awareness step is to kind of "start the engine" by focusing attention on the target sound to be learned. It is a very easy step because the teacher tells the children what to do, but the children have the experience of producing the sound and noticing what that's like.

Note: For older students, it is important to use more appropriate words. For example: The words *machine* and *manager* begin with the same sound, the /m/ sound.

Focus of lesson sequence	Procedure
2. Connect the printed letter with the sound the letter represents.	Show children the large letter *m* card. *This is the letter* m. *The letter* m *stands for the /m/ sound in* Mary *and* Mouse. *You say /m/. Each time I touch the letter* m, *say /m/.* (Touch *m* several times.)

Commentary: This is the whole point of the lesson sequence: to look at the written *m* and say /m/, but to do so in more complicated letter environments, for example when several letters are being shown successively. An even more important context is when the letter appears within a word, such as *man* or *ham*. Even though the point of the lesson is to connect a printed letter with its sound, and this is what step 2 does, this is not enough work with the *m* to /m/ relationship to assume learning. Thus, we go on to the next step.

Focus of lesson sequence	Procedure
3. Discriminate among words that begin with /m/ and those that do not.	At this point, students will need their own letter *m* card. *If the word I say begins with the /m/ sound, hold up your m card and say /m/. If it doesn't begin with the /m/ sound, shake your head number* Example words include: *monkey, many, house, make, table,* and *money.*

Commentary: Step 3 provides another opportunity to identify the /m/ phoneme at the beginning of words and to say /m/ in the presence of the letter *m*.

Note: Here I'd like to remind teachers of young children to use their skills and knowledge of children to make the step above and the other steps fun. For example, in the step above, sometimes you could ask the children to lock their lips if the word does not begin with /m/, or put the *m* card behind their backs if the word does not begin with *m*. The secret to keeping attention is to vary slightly how children respond, but not to overwhelm the point of the step by adding too many variations.

Focus of lesson sequence	Procedure
4. Develop phonemic awareness of the target sound in the final position.	*I am used to sweep the floor. What am I?* After *broom* is said and repeated several times, explain that *broom* ends with the letter *m*, the letter that stands for the /m/ sound. Say some more words that end with the letter *m*, and have students repeat them. Example words include: *jam, room, drum,* and *farm.*

Commentary: Notice how soon the sequence of steps moves to the target in the final position. This is because one of the important principles underlying the instructional procedures here is that children learn that a given letter represents the same sound in any position in words. Recall the McCandliss and others (2003) data that children with inadequate decoding capability decode final graphemes correctly only 54% of the time.

Focus of lesson sequence	Procedure
5. Discriminate among words that end with /m/ from those that do not.	This step is just like step 3, but the focus is on the final position. *I'll say some words. If the word ends with the /m/ sound, hold up your m card. If it doesn't end with the /m/ sound, put your m card behind your back.* *Example words include: ham, tree, broom, dream, drink,* and *drum.*

Commentary: As noted, this step is the same as Step 3, with the focus changed to the /m/ in final position. As such, it provides another opportunity to identify the /m/ at the end of words and to say /m/ in the presence of the letter *m*.

Focus of lesson sequence	Procedure
6. Discriminate among words that have /m/ in the initial and final positions.	Students will need their Word Pockets. *I'll say some words that begin with /m/ and some that end with /m/. When a word begins with /m/, put your letter m at the beginning of the Word Pocket. When a word ends with /m/, put your letter m at the end of the Word Pocket.* *Some examples include: mix, drum, him, money, swim, milk, mouse,* and *ham.*

Commentary: In addition to providing children with practice noticing whether a word begins or ends with /m/, the requirement that they place their *m* letter at the beginning or end of their Word Pocket connects the phonemic position with the visual position.

If *m* is in the initial position of the word:

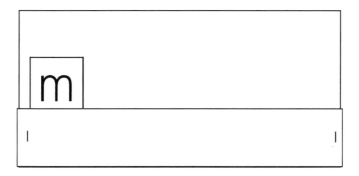

If *m* is in the final position of the word:

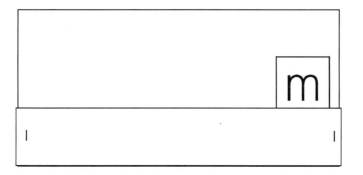

The six steps above, and the many example words to which each step can be applied provide quite extensive instruction. For children who catch on easily, first reduce the number of example words in steps 3 and 5. Subsequently, steps 3 and 5 can be omitted. Finally, reduce the number of example words in the remaining steps.

The above steps can be used for the following consonants:

b as in *bat*   k as in *kid*   s as in *sit*
c as in *can*   l as in *let*   t as in *tan*
d as in *den*   m as in *man*   v as in *vase*
f as in *fox*   n as in *nut*   w as in *wide*
g as in *get*   p as in *pin*   y as in *yard*
h as in *hat*   r as in *ran*   z as in *zoo*
j as in *jump*

The steps are also appropriate for the consonant digraphs below. When teaching consonant digraphs, the letters should be on one card and children should simply be told that the letters *ch,* for example, represent the /ch/ sound in words like *chin* and *chair.*

ch as in *cheese*
sh as in *ship*
th as in *thin*
wh as in *when*

LESSON SEQUENCE FOR TEACHING SHORT-VOWEL LETTER–SOUND CORRESPONDENCE

The six steps for introducing short vowels that follow on pages 39–41 are the same as those for consonants; however, instead of moving from initial position to final position, the sequence for short vowels goes from initial position to medial position. More attention is provided to the medial position. Commentaries are provided only if there is something different for vowels than for the corresponding consonant letter–sound step.

A Sample Lesson Sequence for Teaching the Letter–Sound Correspondence for *a* /a/

Focus of lesson sequence	Procedure
1. Develop phonemic awareness of the target sound in the initial position.	Provide several strong examples of words that being with the target sound: *ant, apple*. Have children repeat each word. Tell children the words begin with the /a/ sound. Ask children to say /a/ several times.

Focus of lesson sequence	Procedure
2. Connect the printed letter with the sound the letter represents.	Show children a large letter *a* card. Say the letter name. Tell children that the letter *a* stands for the /a/ sound in the target words: *ant* and *apple*. Tell children to say /a/ each time you touch the *a* letter.

Focus of lesson sequence	Procedure
3. Discriminate among words that begin with /a/ and those that do not.	Students will need their own *a* letter cards. Have children show their *a* letter card and say /a/ when you say a word that begins with /a/ and put a finger over their lips when a word does not start with the /a/ sound. Some examples include: *animal, answer, window, glass, ant, dog,* and *ambulance*.

Focus of lesson sequence	Procedure
4. Develop phonemic awareness of the target sound in the medial position.	Tell children there are a lot of words that have the /a/ sound in the middle. *I'll say some words that have the /a/ sound in the middle—like* baat *and* caan. *You say them after me and stretch out the /a/ as I do:* caat, jaam, maan, snaap, glaad. *This time when I say a word, I won't stretch out the /a/ sound, but listen for the /a/. First I'll say a word, and then you say it:* jam, man, snap, glad, hat.

Commentary: Identifying a vowel phoneme in the middle of a word is much more difficult than doing so at the beginning of a word. This is because in speech, phonemes often overlap with the previous phoneme (i.e., we begin saying the /a/ sound in *bat* while a remnant of /b/ is present). Thus, I recommend stretching out the vowel sound on the first encounter.

Focus of lesson sequence	Procedure
5. Discriminate among words that have a medial /a/ from those that do not.	*I'll say some words that have the /a/ sound in the middle and some words that do not have the /a/ in the middle. Hold up your a card and say /a/ if you hear a word that has /a/ in the middle. Close your eyes if the word does not have the /a/ sound.* Example words include: *baath, buus, maap, taan, hiip, paast, choomp,* and *chaamp.* Do another round in which the words are said naturally.

Commentary: Notice the recommendation to stretch out the vowel phoneme during the first round. This may be especially important as the children will be discriminating among several medial vowel phonemes, which are articulated in close speech proximity to each other.

Focus of lesson sequence	Procedure
6. Discriminate among words that have /a/ in the initial and medial positions.	*This time when you hear a word that begins with /a/, put your letter a at the beginning of the Word Pocket. When you hear a word that has /a/ in the middle, put your letter a in the middle of your Word Pocket.* *Examples include: apple, tap, ant, sad, band, ask, ran, ashes, fan, and fast.*
Note: Depending on how students respond, you may want to stretch out the /a/, especially in the medial position, and then do another round in which the words are said naturally.	

If *a* is in the initial position of the word:

If *a* is in the medial position of the word:

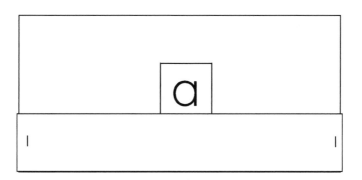

The procedures above are applicable to all the short vowels: *a, e, i, o, u*. Note that it is important that students practice discriminating among letter–sound correspondences. After several letters have been introduced, do quick game-like activities where you show each letter and ask for the sound. As students accumulate more letter–sound correspondences, continue the games with small sets of letters that include the newer letters and some earlier ones and both consonants and vowels.

■ YOUR TURN ■

Identify several students in your classroom or a colleague's classroom who do not know or are weak in their knowledge of consonant and short-vowel letter–sound correspondences. Do a very quick check to identify several correspondences that are unknown. A check can be just a list, not in alphabetical order, of consonants and short vowels for which you ask children to say the sound. Depending on the time of the year and the grade, you may have this information from the results of formal tests. Choose three correspondences to teach the children. For younger children, it would be best to use two consonants and one vowel; for older students, one consonant and two vowels will probably give you better information. It is not wise to teach the short *e* and short *i* in the same lesson as their articulation is in close proximity to each other.

Make the letter cards and use the procedures above to teach the letter–sound correspondences. After instruction, assess learning by showing the children each letter and asking that they produce the sound. Then ask yourself:

1. Did the children learn all the correspondences? If not, why not? Do you need to go over all of them again? Do you need to go over one that seems to be getting mixed up?
2. What did you observe about your ability to present the procedures? How did the students respond? Is there something you need to do more smoothly? Did your pace provide an active lesson?

LESSON SEQUENCE FOR TEACHING THE CORRESPONDENCE FOR TWO-LETTER GRAPHEMES AND THEIR PHONEMES

The goal of the sample lesson that follows below is for a child to be able to look at two-letter graphemes and say the speech sound that the letters represent (e.g., vowel digraphs, diphthongs, and *r*-controlled vowels). The procedures are also appropriate for phonograms as well as other pronounceable units that are represented by more than one letter. The steps in the lesson for teaching correspondences for phonemes represented by multiple letters are:

1. Connect a two-letter grapheme with the phoneme the letters represent.
2. Connect the printed letters with the phoneme the letters represent.
3. In cases when two two-letter graphemes represent the same phoneme, connect both graphemes with the phoneme (e.g., both *ea* and *ee* can represent the long-*e* phoneme).
4. Discriminate among words that may be competitive with target graphemes.

A Sample Lesson for Teaching the Correspondence for Two-Letter Graphemes and Their Phonemes

On pages 44–46, using the *ee* as in *seed* and the *ea* as in *meat* as an example, the steps for teaching two two-letter graphemes that represent the same phoneme are provided.

Focus of lesson sequence	Procedure

1. Connect *ee* to long *e*.	Make the word *seed* in the pocket chart with letter cards. Read the word, and ask the children to read it. Explain that when there are two *e*'s together in a word, they stand for the long-*e* sound, the sound they hear in the middle of *seed*.
	
	    Remove the *s* and the *d*. Tell students to say /ee/ when you touch the letters *ee*.
	
	    Return the *s* and *d* and read *seed*. Ask children to read the word or say the sound as you run your finger under the word or point to the two *e*'s. Go back and forth between *seed* and *ee*.

Commentary: Notice that the new grapheme first appears in a word, and then is pulled out of the word. One reason that I prefer to start with a word is that in typical letter–sound sequences, vowel digraphs are introduced after the short vowels. In order not to insert confusion between, for instance, one *e* and two *ee*'s, I think it wise to provide the new letter sound in a strong visually presented word before dealing with it in isolation.

s	ee	d

ee

Focus of lesson sequence	Procedure
2. Connect *ea* to long *e*.	Make the word *meat* in the pocket chart with letter cards. Read the word, and ask the children to read it. Explain that when *e* and *a* are together in a word, they sometimes represent the long-*e* sound, the sound in the middle of *meat*. Remove the *m* and the *t*. Tell students to say /ee/ when you touch the letters *ea*. Return the *m* and *t* and read *meat*. Ask children to read the word or say the sound as you run your finger under the word or point to *ea*. Go back and forth between *meat* and *ea*.

Focus of lesson sequence	Procedure
3. Connect *ea* and *ee* to long /e/.	Put *seed* and *meat* one under the other in a pocket chart. Have students practice reading both words, making the point that *ea* and *ee* both can stand for the long-*e* sound in words like *seed* and *meat*.

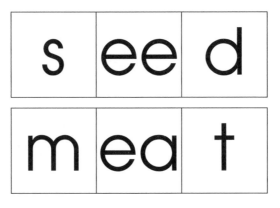

Focus of lesson sequence	Procedure
4. Discriminate among words that may be competitive with *ea* and *ee* words.	Write the words *meat, eat, see, seat, set, sat, meat, met, mat, bee, bet,* and *flea.* Ask the children to read the words.

Commentary: Short-*a* and short-*e* words are included in the list above as a means of requiring students to deal with the vowels in the words. That is, if all the words were long-*e* words, students would be less likely to process the vowels. Note that in Appendix C there are sequences of words that contrast long-vowel digraphs with their potentially competitive short vowels.

■ YOUR TURN ■

As a means of getting comfortable with teaching vowel phonemes that are represented by multiple spellings, it might be useful for you to develop an instructional sequence for teaching the *ay* in *day* and the *ai* in *rain*. The framework for teaching *ee* and *ea* is appropriate for teaching *ay* and *ai*.

INTRODUCING LONG VOWELS OF THE CVCe PATTERN

Over the years, I have come to the conclusion that the most useful way of presenting the CVC*e* pattern (consonant–vowel–consonant–*e*) is simply to demonstrate what happens when an *e* is put at the end of particular CVC words (*hid* to *hide, mat* to *mate*). My preference is to acknowledge the silent-*e* "rule" but to put the instructional emphasis on children engaging in the rule, that is, changing *can* to *cane, cane* to *can, tub* to *tube,* and the like. In Appendices A, B, C, and D, there are sequences of words that provide ways to engage students in using the rule.

MY FAVORITE LETTER–SOUND ANECDOTE

Many years ago, while I was pursuing my PhD, I worked part time at the University of Pittsburgh's Learning Research and Development Center, where I was engaged in a project to develop a reading program that would allow children to proceed at their own rate. A colleague and I (Beck & Mitroff, 1972) went out to a kindergarten class in May, gave the teacher an *m* letter card, and asked her to teach the *m* to /m/ relationship. We audiotaped the lesson.

The teacher held up the *m* letter card and said: "This is an *m*. The name of the letter is *m*, but the sound is /m/ as in *mmmountain*. I want to hear everyone say it."

One child said *m*, two said /m/. Another said *mmmountain*. The teacher said, "No, I want you to say the sound. Listen: /m/ as in *mmmountain, mmmother, mmonkey*. Who can think of another /m/ word?"

Hands went up. One child said, "*Mary*, like my name." A second child said, "We went to the mountains once. It was our vacation. We slept in a tent."

With so many concepts floating about, it seemed clear that not all the children would have understood that the letter *m* represents the /m/ sound in speech. So we developed a very simple instructional procedure: go from the letter name to the letter itself. We tried it out with another teacher.

The teacher held up the *m* card and said, "The name of this letter is *m*. You say the name. The *m* stands for the /m/ sound at the beginning of the word *make*. I'll point to the letter, and I'll say its sound."

She pointed and said /m/ several times and then put the card down in front of one child and said, "You point to the letter, and you say its sound." And the child replied, "Its sound."

The moral of this story is that all the best-laid plans can go awry, especially with children!

4

BLENDING

This chapter builds on the concepts presented in Chapter 3, letter–sounds. After children have learned some letter–sound correspondences for consonants and at least one vowel, they are ready to read some simple words. Learning how to blend will allow them to do that.

A crucial component of being able to decode printed words to speech is being able to blend the sounds in a word together. The importance of blending was emphasized in the National Reading Panel's (2000) report, which stated that "programs that focus too much on the teaching of letter–sound relationships and not enough on putting them to use are unlikely to be very effective" (p. 10).

Let me discuss two important issues associated with blending. First, the traditional admonition about teaching children to blend is that most English phonemes, particularly certain consonants, cannot be produced in isolation without the addition of a schwa. For example, in uttering the phoneme for *c*, one can't really say /c/; one will add the schwa and say /cuh/. Therefore, if a child were asked to blend the phonemes for *c, a*, and *t*, she would produce /cuhatuh/. Let me assert, however, that even if the word *cat* were read in isolation, a child who had any knowledge of what reading is about would not be satisfied with /cuhatuh/. And with any kind of context, it would indeed be a rare child who read "dogs and /cuhatuhs/."

When children attempt to figure out a word by blending sounds, it is not necessary for them to produce a perfect pronunciation. Rather, they need to be able to come up with an approximate pronunciation, which they can refine by matching their pronunciation with a word they already know from spoken language. Even as adults, we sometimes need to do that; I do it with medical and pharmaceutical terms, for example. That is, I know some pharmaceutical terms from having heard them said out loud in a physician's office or in drugstores, but upon first seeing such a term in print, I may pronounce it roughly. However, if I can match it with an oral term, I refine it. In particular, I am thinking of when I asked a pharmacist what the ingredient in cold medicines that can cause some people to become jittery was. He told me that it was pseudoephedrine, and I repeated it.

In the course of writing this book, I learned from the newspaper that pseudoephedrine was being abused by some. When I read *pseudoephedrine* in the newspaper (the first time I had ever seen it in print), my inner speech rendition of the word was wobbly until I recognized that I knew the oral version and was able to refine my approximation with the word in my spoken repertoire and pronounce it properly.

The second issue about blending is that it can be quite difficult for young readers to get the hang of it. In this regard, I have long been interested in the lack of instruction that children receive about how to blend words. In the late 1970s, my conclusion about four programs that labeled themselves code-emphasis programs was that only two dealt with blending in any way whatsoever (Beck & McCaslin, 1978). Today, I would say that I gave too much credit to those two programs because I don't think that the approaches really taught children what to do when they needed to put phonemes together to pronounce a word. The problem in those older materials was not that the instructional strategies for blending were not working. The problem was that there was a virtual absence of any useful instructional strategy. The teacher's editions essentially told the teacher to say something like "Stretch out the sounds and blend them together." *How* to "blend them together" is the problematic link.

Is blending taught better now? Yes and no. Sometimes I see teachers asking children to imitate the teacher's rendition of stretching out the sounds. Imitation is a good first step, but instruction has to go further if children are to learn to apply blending independently. What I have seen more often is final blending, which is similar to being asked to stretch out the sounds. That is, teachers ask children to say each sound in a word (/c/ /a/ /t/) and then to blend the three sounds. The problem with final blending is that one has to keep three meaningless phonemes in short-term memory and then blend them. Three is hard enough, but think how hard it would be to keep four or five meaningless phonemes in memory: /c/ /r/ /u/ /s/ /t/. It is virtually impossible for a beginning reader. The example of *crust* was provided only to make the point to adults that holding multiple phonemes in short-term memory is difficult. As an aside, I would expect that by the time a young reader encountered *crust,* she would have moved beyond needing to blend all the sounds overtly.

In contrast to final blending, I strongly recommend successive blending (which I have sometimes called cumulative blending). In successive blending, students say the first two sounds in a word and immediately blend those two sounds together. Then they say the third sound and immediately blend that sound with the first two blended sounds. If it is a four-phoneme word, then they say the fourth phoneme and immediately blend that sound with the first three blended sounds. The strong advantage of successive blending is that it is less taxing for short-term memory because blending occurs immediately after each new phoneme is pronounced. As such, at no time must more than two sounds be held in memory (the sound immediately produced and the one that directly precedes it), and at no time must more than two sound units be blended.

Consider what *crust* would be like if an individual were using successive blending.

/c/   /r/   /c̲r̲/   /u/   /c̲r̲u̲/   /s/   /c̲r̲u̲s̲/   /t/   c̲r̲u̲s̲t̲

The underlined portions show where blending occurs and displays that no more than two sounds need to be held in short-term memory.

Is the memory factor in blending really a big problem? After all, first-grade children normally have a memory span that can easily encompass three elements (as shown, for example, by the digit-span test of the Stanford–Binet, which expects memory of three digits at age 3, five at age 7). Tests such as the digit span, however, require only that the items that an examiner provides be held in memory. Items need not be generated, and no competing processing interferes with retention. This is not the case during decoding. A substantial amount of other processing (i.e., putting the sounds together) must occur simultaneously with the retention of the phoneme elements. This additional processing is likely to interfere with remembering the sounds or rehearsal of the sounds may interfere with other processing.

Given the issues above, I developed a very ritualized procedure for teaching blending, in which physical actions accompany the oral blending. The notion was that the physical action could provide a kind of external representation of what goes on during the blending process.

For example, in the case of the word *cat,* the child who was performing the blending procedure independently would:

1. Point to the *c* and say /c/.
2. Point to the *a* and say /a/.
3. Slide his finger under the *ca* and say /ka/.
4. Point to the *t* and say /t/.
5. Slide his finger under *cat* and say /cat/ slowly.
6. Read the word naturally, and indicate that the word is *cat.*

The point of teaching children to blend is that they have a procedure in their repertoire that they can call on if they need to. Once a child can independently engage in the steps of learning a new word, there is no need for the child to continue to blend words overtly. Blending is a little like the saying "A little salt is good; too much is not healthy." Once children can demonstrate that they know the procedure, they do not need to engage in it routinely.

However, as a way of keeping blending available in children's repertoires, I have seen teachers occasionally fold blending into an activity to check decoding. Specifically I am thinking of the time I observed a small group session that a first-grade teacher arranged for several children who seemed to be floundering in a particular whole-class lesson. That one child was having difficulty with words ending in *g* was clearly shown when he read *dot* for *dog* (earlier he had read *hot* for *hog*). In the small group session, the teacher pointed to *dog* and asked the child to blend it. When he got to step 4 above and pointed to the *g*, he looked sideways at his teacher. She smiled, and he said /g/, and proceeded to read *dog.* This time when he looked sideways, he smiled at the teacher. Then, they both laughed.

TEACHING SUCCESSIVE BLENDING

Materials

To teach the lessons for successive blending, you will need the following materials:

- Large letter cards for your use during instruction
- Pocket chart for displaying large letter cards
- A set of individual letter cards for each student

Lesson Sequences for Teaching Successive Blending

The intention of the procedures below is to *introduce* children to blending by having children watch you as you do a step and then having them do that step.

Place your letters in a pocket chart with spaces between them.

(s . . . a . . . t)

Have students place their cards on their desks in the same way.

s a	Point to the letters one at a time and say /s/ . . . /a/. Then, tell the students to point to their letters and say the sounds with you as you say them again.
sa	Slide the letter *a* over to the *s*. Run your finger under the *sa* and say: "/sa/ . . . /sa/."
s a	Then move the *a* back to where it was.
sa	Tell students to slide their letter *a* over to the *s* and to slide their finger under the *sa* and say /sa/ as you do the same with your cards.
sa t	Slide your finger under the *sa*. Say /sa/, holding the sound until you point to the *t* and say /t/. Have students do the same with their letters.
sat	Move the *t* over to the *sa*. Slide your finger under the *sat* and say, "/sat/. This word is *sat*." Move the *t* back to its original position. Have students move their *t* over to the *sa* and read /sat/.

The techniques for teaching the blending procedure include a series of steps that lead the child from imitating the procedure to performing it independently. Essentially, the teacher repeats the linking and blending of sounds three times. At each repetition, the teacher systematically fades out of the process and gives greater responsibility to the child. At the end of the sequence, the child demonstrates the procedure by himself.

1. The teacher models the blending procedure. She models the sounds and the blends and uses finger-pointing procedures and intermittent verbal directions.
2. The children imitate the model while the teacher repeats both the verbal cues and the finger cues to assist them.
3. The teacher repeats the procedure, but this time does not model the sounds or the blends. She gives only the verbal cues and the finger cues to assist.
4. The procedure is repeated. This time, the teacher drops the verbal cues. She gives only finger cues (i.e., the prompts are faded).
5. The child performs the pointing, sounding, and blending steps.

As noted, the detailed procedures above are provided to introduce children to successive blending. Based on my own observations and, conservatively, hundreds and hundreds of teachers' comments, most children have been able to learn the chain and, even more important, have been able to use the steps to figure out new words. Also very important is their eventual ability to shorten the steps by collapsing four steps into two (e.g., /m/ /ast/).

A strong advantage of the successive blending chain is the precise information available to the teacher in terms of locating an error. If a child makes an error while performing the chain, the teacher knows where the error is—that is, which link in the chain is incorrect. With this kind of precise information, the teacher can give the child a direct prompt. For example, if a child's inability to develop a correct candidate pronunciation of a word was caused by a substituted or omitted phoneme, the teacher could point to the letter and ask the child to say the phoneme. If the child does not provide the phoneme, the teacher could prompt the sound with a silent mouthing cue (showing what the mouth looks like when the phoneme is uttered). For example, when blending the phonemes in *black*, if the child said /b/ /a/, the teacher could point to the *l*, ask for the sound, and if needed provide a silent mouthing cue or the sound. I chose this particular example because it is the case that the second consonant in an initial consonant blend and the first consonant in a final consonant blend have a high error rate (McCandliss et al., 2003).

As another example, if a child made an error in the blending of the first two letters in *set* and said /sa/, the teacher could run her finger under the *se* and ask the child to say the sound of the two letters together. The availability of precise error information enables the teacher to go right into where the problem is and deal with it. This is in contrast to simply knowing that a child didn't read *black* or *set* correctly.

■ YOUR TURN ■

Try to find a situation in which you can teach a student to blend. The only prerequisite is that the child know the letter–sound correspondences for three consonants and a vowel that can be combined into at least two words. For example: *m, a, n,* and *t* would allow *man, mat, tan,* and *tam; m, a, s,* and *d* would allow *mad, sad, dam,* and *sam.* It is a good idea first to practice the procedures with an adult.

MY FAVORITE BLENDING ANECDOTE

When working out the blending procedure and the chain of prompt, I tried the steps out with first-grade children early in the school year. I observed one child who the teacher had told me had just caught on to the procedures and was independently pointing and engaging in the steps. I had noticed that in the course of pointing the child was pressing his finger quite hard. The child was slow and deliberate and seemed to be giving birth to the word as a colleague who saw him suggested. He completed the steps perfectly and then raised his hand, shook it up and down (the way you might when you've been writing for a long time), and said, "Whew!" My colleague asked, "What's the matter? Are you tired?" The child replied, "No, my finger is hot."

5

WORD BUILDING

This chapter deals with Word Building, an activity that supports decoding and word recognition by giving students opportunities consistently to experience and discriminate the effects on a word of changing one letter. As such, the procedures require students to focus attention on every letter in the sequences of letters that make up words. This helps students "see" and develop a sense of English orthography.

Developing a sense of how English works is a very important component of reading acquisition. Good readers have a sense of English orthography, which may be explicit or implicit. But in either case, if you saw a word that started with *btrz,* you would not identify it as an English word. Or when you see a simple word like *train,* you know instantly that without the *t,* the word is *rain.* You also know that if the letters *s* and *p* were put in front of *rain,* the word would be *sprain.* These examples are simply instances of your sense of the way written English words. And because you have such a sense about words, when you read you are able to concentrate on the ideas you are reading about, not the individual works. Word Building helps students develop this sense of how written English works as well as the details of many spelling patterns.

Word Building lessons are sequences of words in which there is progressive minimal contrast from word to word. That is, given a first word, each subsequent word is different from the previous word by one letter (e.g., *man, can, cat, hat, hit, hid, had*). Within each Word Building sequence, children are given a small set of letter cards and directed by the teacher to form a word (e.g., *hit*) and read it. Then the teacher instructs children to exchange a letter, delete a letter, or insert a letter, which transforms the current word into the next word in a lesson sequence (e.g., *him*). To be successful, children need to pay attention to all the letters in a word.

Being able to attend to all the letters in a word represents full alphabetic decoding, which contrasts with partial alphabetic decoding (Ehri, 1999). In the latter, children might apply their letter–sound knowledge to some of the letters in a novel word but not to each of the letters in it. How many of us have heard children read *hat* for *hit, ran* for *rain, back* for *black,* and the like?

The advantage of full alphabetic knowledge goes beyond correctly reading *hit, rain,* and *black.* Several theorists have suggested that full alphabetic decoding plays a role in a self-teaching process (Ehri, 1999; Perfetti, 1985; Share & Stanovich, 1995). The self-teaching process suggests that engaging in a correct but perhaps belabored process may support more sophisticated performance in the process. With this in mind, Share (1995) made the point that engagement in alphabetic decoding may serve as a bootstrapping or self-help mechanism that helps readers progress from early attempts to pronounce novel words toward accurate identification of familiar words in ways that capture the important orthographic content that is necessary for accurate and fluent word recognition.

Empirical results of the use of Word Building are quite positive. In the McCandliss and others (2003) intervention mentioned earlier, children who had inadequate reading skills after 1–3 years of schooling engaged in Word Building for 20 sessions. Compared to a matched control group, children in the Word Building group made significantly greater progress on standardized tests of decoding, comprehension, and phonological awareness.

THE WORD BUILDING SEQUENCES

Word Building sequences are divided into four categories (see Appendices A, B, C, and D). The A category deals with consonants, short vowels, consonant blends, and consonant digraphs. The B category focuses on long vowels of the CVC*e* pattern. The C category focuses on long-vowel digraphs and emphasizes vowel pairs that have the same phoneme (e.g., *seed* and *meat*; *rain* and *day*). The sequences in the D category deal with some *r*-controlled vowels.

The sequences in each of the categories are divided into units. Units comprise three related sequences. For example, in the A category, the three sequences below make up Unit 2.

A4	**A5**	**A6**
sat	hit	ham
sit	hid	him
a, i, s, t	a, d, h, i, s, t	a, d, d, h, i, m, t
sit	hid	ham
sat	had	him
at	sad	hit
it	sat	hid
sit	sit	had
sat	hat	ham
sit	at	him
	it	dim
	hit	did
		dad

The content of the sequences is discussed in the Appendices. Here I turn to the procedures for presenting Word Building.

PROCEDURES FOR BUILDING WORDS

The words in sequence A5 will be used to illustrate the procedures.

A5
hit
hid
a, d, h, i, s, t
hid
had
sad
sat
hat
at
it
hit

Materials

- Large letter cards for the six letters shown.
- Pocket chart for displaying large letter cards.
- A set of individual letter cards for each student. Note that for some lessons, children will need more than one copy of some letters.
- Individual Word Pockets for each student for sorting and displaying letters.
- Individual letters that can be laminated and duplicated for each child and directions for making Word Pockets are in Appendix F.

Student Letter Cards

Before the lesson begins, students should place their letter cards, in this case (*a, d, h, i, s, t*) above their Word Pockets.

Demonstration

The first two words in each sequence are intended for teacher demonstration. The teacher starts a lesson by making the first word, *hit,* in the Pocket chart, reading the word, asking the children to read it, and telling them that she is going to change one letter and make a new word.

> "This is the word *hit*. Read the word with me. (*hit*) I'm going to change one letter in *hit* to make a new word."

Change the *t* in *hit* to *d* and have students read the word. (*hid*)

Words Students Build

Tell the students that it's their turn to build words and that you will tell them which letters to use.

> "Now you can build words. I'll tell you what letters to use. Put the letter *h* in the beginning. Put the letter *i* after the *h*. Put the letter *d* at the end of the word. What is the word?" (*hid*)

Continue by having students change letters and having each word read aloud.

1. "Put letter *a* between *h* and *d*. What word did you make?" (*had*)
2. "Change the *h* to *s*. What's the word?" (*sad*)
3. "Change the *d* to *t*. What's the word?" (*sat*)
4. "Change the *s* to *h*. What's the word?" (*hat*)
5. "Take away the *h*. What word is left?" (*at*)
6. "Change the *a* to *i*. What's the word?" (*it*)
7. "Put an *h* before the *i*. What's the word?" (*hit*)

As each word is made write it in a column on the board, and when the sequence is complete have the column of words read.

These same procedures can be applied with occasional minor differences to all the Word Building sequences.

WHAT'S SO DIFFERENT ABOUT WORD BUILDING?

It is the case that teachers have been engaging in letter substitution for decades, in the forms of word wheels and flip books. It has been my experience, however, that often teachers develop phonics word wheels or flip books that tend not to put attention where it is needed (i.e. on what is a new or difficult phonic element). Think about a word wheel that a teacher developed to bring attention to the newly introduced short-*i* vowel sound. In the word wheel, the *i* remained constant and the initial consonant changed (e.g., *hit, pit, sit*). Then the final consonant was changed (*him, hit, hid*). This was done because the teacher's belief was that by continually showing the *i* and asking that words with the short-*i* vowel sound be read, the short *i* would be reinforced. Certainly this is not all wrong and may be a reasonable first step. The caveat, however, is that if the vowel sound is always the short *i*, then students' attention needs to be focused on consonants but not so much on the *i* because if all the words have the *i* vowel, there is little need to process the *i*.

ATTENTION TO WHAT IS NEW

If the content goal of a lesson is to know, for instance, the *i* to /i/ relationship, then the new vowel should be contrasted with at least one other vowel. Again, this is because we want children to process the *i* to /i/ relationship, and without discriminating it from another vowel, it is not clear that much learning will take place.

Relatedly, if the content goal is to add a new consonant letter–sound relationship to a child's repertoire, then the consonants should change so that the child needs to discriminate among newly introduced and previously introduced consonants. Thus, the idea of substituting letters to form words has been around for some time. But traditionally such activities are not done consistently, and attention may not be given to what it is that the letter-substitution activity is to focus on.

ATTENTION TO ALL LETTERS IN A WORD

As noted earlier, children who have difficulty with decoding tend not to pay attention to all the letters in a word. Full alphabetic decoding requires attention to all the letters in a word. The progressive minimal contrast activity—one letter changes and a new word results—inherent in Word Building requires students to do this. This scaffolds the process of decoding each letter position within a word, especially the positions that children may ignore: the final and medial position.

MORE ATTENTION TO VOWELS

There is a lot of evidence that the vowels in English are difficult. Therefore, in the Word Building sequences, a lot of attention to the vowels is required. In many sequences, there are words that are different from one another only in the vowel. Thus, as children engage in the Word Building sequences, they will need to pay attention to the vowels.

SPIRALING SEQUENCES

The sequences in Word Building were built in a cumulative, spiraling way. The consonant blends are an example. Consonant blends that can appear in a sequence after each of the single consonants in that blend have been included. For example, when previous sequences have included the *s* and the *t*, the *st* blend can be made available. Word Building is very helpful for supporting the reading of consonant blends because, for example, children get to experience reading *top*, putting an *s* in front of *top* and reading the resultant *stop*, or reading *cost*, taking away the *s* and reading *cot*. There is evidence that children make more mistakes on the second letter in an initial blend (e.g., the *p* in *spot*) than the first letter and more mistakes on the first letter in a final blend (e.g., the *s* in *cast*) than on the last letter (McCandliss et al., 2003). Word Building brings attention to such ins and outs of English orthography.

WHERE SHOULD WORD BUILDING BEGIN?

Where a teacher begins depends on where the child is. If you are working with beginning readers, you can probably begin with the A1 sequence. However, you may not want to go through all of the A sequences before you start some of the B sequences. All the short vowels have been introduced by A22, so you might want to start introducing the long CVC*e* pattern in the B sequences. Many of the B sequences include discrimination between the short vowels and long vowels, but you may want to add more. If you are working with an older child who is having difficulty, try several of the earlier sequences and look for the places where the child gets some words right but tends to get mixed-up. Work with the child on those partly right/partly mixed-up sequences.

WHAT DO I DO
WHEN CHILDREN MAKE MISTAKES?

An important teaching opportunity exists when a child misreads a word. The major teaching device is to show the child the difference between what she read and what should have been read. As an example, suppose your directions said to put *h* at the beginning, *o* in the middle, and *t* at the end, and instead of reading *hot*, a child reads *hat*. Immediately show the child the difference; that is, write the two words vertically

hot

hat

and ask the child to tell you what is different about the two words. There are other ways of correcting and prompting, but a major rule of thumb is to let the child immediately compare her response to the correct response.

DECODING TO ENCODING

As indicated in the procedures, the directions tell the child what letters to put in what place (e.g., put *c* at the beginning, put *a* after *c,* and put *t* at the end). The child is asked to read the word and then instructed to make a change (e.g., take *c* away and put *m* at the beginning. What's the word?). This decoding approach is what is recommended. However, a second way to go through the words in a sequence, especially in later sequences, is to ask the child to identify the letter(s) that will change one word into another. This encoding approach works as follows. First the teacher gives the usual directions to make the first word in a sequence. After the first word has been made and read (e.g., *cat*), the teacher does not tell the students which letter to change; rather, she tells them to change one letter to make *cat* say *mat*. This encoding is especially good in CVC/CVC*e* discriminations. For example, if the first word was *fin,* ask the child to add a letter to make it say *fine*. Although the encoding approach is valuable, I strongly recommend decoding as the initial way to proceed through a sequence.

OTHER WORD BUILDING GAMES AND EXTENSIONS

- Students can keep Word Building journals. At the completion of a Word Building lesson, they can write the words they built and create a few sentences using some of the words.
- Pairs of children can conduct their own Word Building sequences. Individual magnetic letter boards and letters are useful here.

- Children enjoy speed rounds. One way is to keep track of the time it took to complete an initial round and then the time for subsequent rounds.
- When children's writing competence has advanced to where they don't write too slowly, you can do some of the sequences through writing. Ask the children to write numbers in a column on their papers. Tell them the letters to write to produce a first word and have the word read, then tell them the letters to write to produce the second word and have it read, and so on.

MY FAVORITE WORD BUILDING ANECDOTE

I was visiting a first-grade class in March, in which there was a husky boy (let's call him Daryl) who according to the teacher had come to the class several months earlier with few literacy skills, but who was making good progress—largely in thanks to a rather little girl (let's call her Janet) who had taken him under her wing in most things. The teacher had described Janet as a "little mother and little teacher."

I got close enough to watch and hear the two children, who always sat next to each other, during a Word Building lesson. Janet kept an eye on Daryl at each letter exchange and sometimes when he read the word aloud, she patted him on his arm or flashed a smile. And should he bring the wrong letter down, she flashed him a "hmm?" look, and Daryl looked again at his cards. If Daryl wasn't keeping up, Janet pointed to the correct letter.

At the end of the lesson, I said something to Daryl about his doing well. Janet then said something like, "He really is [doing well], but he don't see how many words you can get by changing one letter. But he will!"

6

MULTISYLLABIC WORDS

This chapter focuses on the decoding of multisyllabic words, a logical next step in the sequence of students' developing decoding skills. One of the most interesting misreadings of multisyllabic words was brought to my attention by one of my master's students in a class I taught. Below are some examples of the sixth-grade student's responses.

Word	Student's response
nauseous	nearsiseous
bountiful	beautiful
expected	exited
logical	local
machetes	matches
experiences	expects
culprit	culpit
persist	present
untenable	unable

This student appeared to use the beginning and ending portions of most target words but was virtually at a loss with internal syllables. He either made up an internal syllable (as in *nearsiseous* for *nauseous*), changed an internal syllable (as in *exited* for *expected*), omitted internal syllables (*local* for *logical*, *expects* for *experiences*, *unable* for *untenable*), or changed the target word to a likely known word that had the correct beginnings and endings (*beautiful* for *bountiful*, *present* for *persist*).

I cannot say I had seen such a set of misreadings before I encountered the ones here. I wish I could tell you more about this child, but it was at the end of the semester, and I merely suggested to my student that she have her student make words from syllable cards. That was not too bad a suggestion, but more would certainly have been needed

The decoding of multisyllabic words poses difficulties beyond decoding of single-syllable words. The reader who encounters an unfamiliar multisyllabic word needs to divide the word into pronounceable subunits (often syllables, but not necessarily), so he can work on the pronunciation of the subunits and put those pronunciations together to produce a candidate word.

Let's try to do exactly that with a pseudoword.

■ Divide *obbodious* into pronounceable sub units.

Below is how my friend (let's call him Eric) divided the word.

■ *ob-bod-i-ous*

Now, here's a reconstruction of my conversation with Eric about why he had made his choices.

■ Eric identified *ob* as the first syllable because he thought he "knew" that within multisyllabic words, syllables often fall between two adjacent consonants. He also said, rather assuredly, something like, "I can't think of a word that starts with *obb*." (Interestingly, while writing this book, I quickly looked at the entries in a dictionary, albeit an old *Webster's New Collegiate Dictionary* [1977], for *obb* and found only *obbligato,* "used as a direction in music").

Notice that Eric used two sources to identify *ob*: vague knowledge and lots of experience. The notion that one "knows" something does not necessarily mean that one can provide a rule or rationale.

■ Eric identified *bod* as the second syllable. He indicated that it could be *bo* (the long-vowel sound of *o*), but that *bod* (the short-vowel sound of *o*) "went better with the first syllable, *ob*." That is, he liked *ob-bod*.

My guess is that Eric saw *bod* and preferred that CVC to the open long syllable *bo*. Perhaps, given his wide experience as a reader, Eric unconsciously considered probabilities: are there more CVC second syllables than CV second syllables? I don't know, and I don't know that anyone knows.

■ Given his decision to identify the second syllable as *bod,* Eric had to choose *i* as the third syllable, otherwise the third syllable would have to be *ious,* which, to the best of my knowledge, is infrequent. Interestingly, when he chose *i,* he remarked that there are a lot of words in which a vowel is a syllable.

In that comment Eric demonstrated his knowledge of a major requirement for a syllable: it has to have a vowel.

■ Given Eric's decisions to this point, he had to identify *ous* as the final syllable and he indicated that there are a lot of words that end in *ous.*

So what can be said about what Eric knew and did to divide the word into subunits? He knew that a syllable consists of a letter or several letters that must involve a vowel sound. He was aware that there are several possibilities for the second syllable: either *bod* or *bo.* And here he appeared to be incorporating a sense of accent. That is, should *ob bod i ous* be pronounced with the stress on the first or second syllable? If my memory serves me, when Eric put the syllables together he seemed to have decided that the accent should go on the second syllable (that is, *obBODious* not *OBbodious*).

Such knowledge goes beyond what is needed for decoding single-syllable words because for single-syllable words the vowel environment is given rather than derived by the reader and stress is not an issue.

From my experience of hearing students stumble over multisyllabic words, the student's unusual responses at the beginning of this chapter, Eric's responses to *obbodious,* and some attempted analyses of my own responses to multisyllabic pseudowords (there was a time when I asked friends to provide me with four- and five-syllable pronounceable pseudowords, which I would read into a tape recorder), my conclusion was that supporting students to read multisyllabic words has to involve both analysis and synthesis, and that there needs to be a lot of practice doing both.

To provide opportunities for students to participate in the analysis and synthesis of multisyllabic words, Steve Roth, Margaret McKeown, and I designed Syllasearch. Originally, Syllasearch (Beck, Roth, & McKeown,1985) was implemented as a computer program, which has long been technologically outdated. The procedures, however, were not difficult to adapt to cards (one of the staples in teaching elementary grades).

LESSON SEQUENCE FOR SYLLASEARCH

The words and syllables below are from Medium Set 4 of the Syllasearch Words and Syllables lists found in Appendix E. This set is used to illustrate the procedures.

Materials

- Word cards and syllable cards as indicated above.
- A pocket chart on which all the word and syllable cards can be placed and moved about. Instead of using a pocket chart, you can put "sticky tac" on the back of the cards so they can be placed on a whiteboard or chalkboard and moved around.

Overview

Tell students that they are going to learn to play Syllasearch, which will help them read long words (multisyllabic words) fast and easily. Explain that Syllasearch has three parts.

In the first part, Meet the Words, they will become acquainted with a set of words. "Become acquainted with" means that you will simply read the words in a Syllasearch set aloud, and they can read along with you.

In the second part, Find the Syllables, students will be asked to find syllables within the words.

In the third part, Collect the Words, the syllables that have been identified in Find the Syllables will become the parts that students will use to make words.

Meet the Words

The purpose of Meet the Words is to provide students with a quick overview of the set of words they will use. Display the complete set of word cards in a column in a pocket chart or on sticky cards on a board. Tell students that these are the words that they will use in the game. Go down the column, pointing to each word, reading it aloud, and, if you like, using the words that you think students may not have heard in a very brief sentence or definition-like statement—for example, "*Marvel. Marvel* means to think something is *marvelous* . . . terrific. Somebody might say 'I marvel at how fast a spaceship moves.' " It is very important that you not belabor the meaning of the words and that you keep this part of Syllasearch very brief and fast-paced. The point of Meet the Words is only to provide the students with a context for a set of words that they will deal with in the upcoming game of Syllasearch.

Find the Syllables

Keep the first word from the list, *center,* and remove the others.

"This word is center. Read it with me . . . *center.*"

Ask a student to come to the board and point to the parts of the word as you ask, or point to the letters as you ask the class the following questions.

"What letters stand for the /cen/ sound in *center?*"
"What is the sound the letters *c, e, n* stand for?"

Put the *cen* syllable card on the board.

"What letters stand for the /ter/ sound in *center?*"
"What is the sound the letters *t, e, r* stand for?"

Put the *ter* syllable card on the board.
     The syllable cards need to be arranged on the board or pocket chart in a matrix identical to that on the Syllable Matrix for those words in Appendix E. For example, the syllable card *cen* should appear at the top of the first column of

the matrix that will be developed. The syllable card for *ter* should appear in the second column, second row:

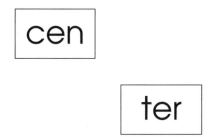

A way to keep track of where the syllable cards go is to put a small code in the corner of each card—for example, on the *cen* card (column 1, row 1) and on the *ter* card (column 2, row 2). When you get to a repeated syllable, (e.g., *mar* will already be on the matrix when the syllables for *marvelous* are requested), point out to the students that the syllable is already on the matrix. The use of one syllable in several words is particularly beneficial.

Below is what the matrix will look like after you have done the first three words:

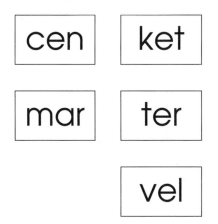

Continue asking students to identify the syllables in each word until all the words have been shown and all the syllable cards are arranged in the matrix:

When the matrix is complete, tell students that all the syllables have been identified, and they are ready to go on to the part of the game called Collect the Words.

Collect the Words

In this part, students collect words by combining syllables from the matrix columns. There are three versions of Collect the Words.

Version 1

Say one of the words (e.g., *marvelous*) and have a student build that word from the syllables in the matrix. The student should take one syllable from each column to build the word, placing the syllable cards below the matrix to form the word. So the display would look like the following:

Have the students read the word that was built from the syllables, then return each of the syllable cards in the word to its place in the matrix. Students can write the word as you write the word on the chalkboard or put the completed word card (not the syllables that make the word) in a column at the far right of the pocket chart, so that the display looks like the following:

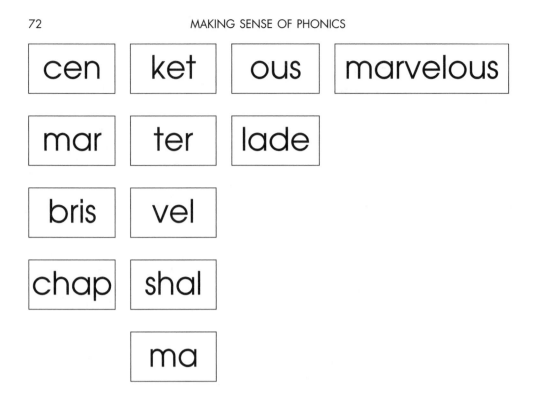

Continue in this same way until all the words have been built, pronounced, and written. At the completion of this version of Collect the Words, the final display should look as follows, with the exception that the list of words can be in any order.

Version 2

This version starts with the matrix. The difference is that instead of you telling the students what word to make, as in Version 1, call on a student to come and make any word she likes, noting that there are eight real words that can be made.

When a word is made, write that word on the chalkboard, or place it in the pocket chart as a way of keeping track of which of the words have been built.

Version 3

This version also starts with the matrix. The difference is that instead of telling a student to make a real word, now you want him to put syllables together that do *not* make a real word and to pronounce the made-up word. Most teachers call these nonsense words (e.g., *chapmalade*). Some teachers and students have developed other names for such words (e.g., alien words, silly words, wacky words). Sometimes teachers ask students what a given word might mean in nonsense word language.

Both teachers and students are quite fond of Syllasearch, and students particularly enjoy Version 3. As it turns out, Version 3 may be the most beneficial of all.

Other Ways of Practicing

1. Have the students make their own sets of syllable cards and follow along in a lesson.
2. Using the matrix on the board as a model, students can arrange the cards in the same formation on their desks and try to build the eight words. They can check their success with the list of words they wrote in Version 1.
3. Ask the students to work in pairs to make some words with the syllables, both real and nonsense words, pronounce them to their partners, and then write them down.
4. There are a variety of game-like overlays that can be applied to Syllasearch, such as keeping track of how fast a student or a pair of students can build all the words in a set. The important point is that repeated practice finding the syllables (analysis of words) and then collecting the words (synthesis of words) will help students tackle new multisyllabic words. It is important, however, that the repeated practices be fun. If they get boring and pedantic, they lose their potential power.
5. Teachers have found it useful to develop sets of words and syllables for multisyllabic words that students will encounter in tradebooks and other materials that they will read.

■ YOUR TURN ■

Select a Syllasearch set from Appendix E. Make the syllable and word cards and use the procedures above to teach a lesson. Then ask yourself:

1. Do you think the students learned anything? If yes, what? If not, why not? Was the Syllasearch set at a good level for the students? Was the set too easy? Too hard? Would it be useful to repeat the lesson?
2.   Reflect on your ability to present the procedures. Are there steps you need to do more smoothly? Have you developed a code for the syllable cards that allows you to keep track of them? Did your pace provide an active lesson? How did the students respond?

MY FAVORITE SYLLASEARCH ANECDOTES

Over the years, teachers have told me about some of the things students say a given nonsense word means. Some of my favorite responses are: *mabrisous* is a thing that could make you sick; *chapmalade* is something that you smear on your skin so your skin feels nice; *brister* is an alien planet. When a fifth grader indicated that *pronoy* meant that "you are annoying someone," the teacher suggested that maybe he had seen a similarity between *annoy* and *pronoy*. The student quickly responded that they were similar, but that *pronoy* was "annoying someone more than just annoying!"

Perhaps my all-time favorite is the student who synthesized four syllables from a matrix and slowly read *procelerble*. When asked what it might mean, the student responded, "I haven't a clue. I'm lucky to just be able to say it!"

EPILOGUE

You've probably all had the experience that while you are doing one thing, something else comes to mind. That certainly happened to me over the course of writing this book. There were three things that came to mind most often. First, I wanted to suggest ways that the instructional strategies I was writing about might be used in various classroom settings. Second, I wanted to emphasize the importance of becoming fluent when using the instructional procedures. Third, and most often, I wanted to underscore that decoding is a necessary but not sufficient condition for becoming a competent reader. Teachers need to keep the other components of reading, especially vocabulary development and comprehension, present and active in their classrooms. So early on, I decided to include this epilogue in which I could briefly discuss these matters.

USING THE INSTRUCTIONAL STRATEGIES IN VARIOUS CLASSROOM SITUATIONS

I have different suggestions for various classroom situations. To begin with, I want to acknowledge that if the instructional approaches in use to teach decoding skills are functioning well, then there may be little reason to engage in the procedures I have suggested in this book. However, even when most of the children in a classroom are acquiring decoding skills adequately, it is far from unique that some children need more instruction. Thus, I present below some of the situations in which the strategies in this book would be useful.

■ **To address individual needs.** Some children simply need more instructional time to learn. Some need to receive additional instruction in small groups or in one-to-one tutoring situations. The procedures in this book can be used effectively with such children.

■ **To supplement decoding instruction.** It is often the case that commercial programs provide the same amount of instruction for letter–sound correspondences that are not the same in terms of difficulty; for example, the *m* to /m/ relationship and the short *o* to /o/. The former is easier to recall than the latter, especially when other vowels are part of the accumulating sequence. Thus, the procedures for teaching letter–sound correspondences presented in this book should be useful to supplement those presented in the commercial program.

■ **To teach blending.** Some programs in use in primary classrooms do not actually teach children how to blend. That is, the instructional suggestion only requires that children repeat the teacher's model. As noted earlier, blending can be tricky to teach. The blending chain provided in this book was developed to overcome difficulties in teaching and learning blending.

■ **To provide practice toward building automaticity.** If children's word recognition is accurate but slow, speed rounds with Word Building can be helpful.

■ **To provide systematic phonics instruction.** Some approaches used in classrooms do not include explicit, systematic phonics. Rather, "opportunistic" phonics—pointing out phonic elements in the course of reading little books—is the major approach. As I write this book, it is the case that Reading First classrooms must use an approach that includes explicit, systematic phonics. But there are a huge number of non-Reading First classrooms, many of which do not use explicit, systematic phonics. The procedures and materials provided in this book would be very useful in such situations.

■ **To support spelling instruction.** If children's spelling is not adequate, practice with Word Building is very useful.

■ **To support multisyllabic decoding.** The procedures in Chapter 6 are useful for decoding words longer than one single syllable.

Beyond uses of various strategies in classrooms, it is my hope that the explanations I have provided about the role of decoding in reading and the teaching of decoding will enhance teachers' understanding. If that is the case, then they will be able to make decisions about when and how to use the strategies most effectively with their students.

BECOMING FLUENT WITH THE INSTRUCTIONAL PROCEDURES

In the course of writing this book, I presented a workshop to teachers about letter–sound instruction, blending, and Word Building. It had been more than several years since I was in a situation to demonstrate the strategies on my own (usually teachers who work with the procedures do so). My demonstrations were far from smooth—I was rusty in moving cards, recalling the next step, and the like. I was perfectly able to explain the theory and research of the strategies—after all, they were ones I had developed—but I was somewhat clumsy in demonstrating them. I was out of practice.

Most teachers have told me that it took a little time until they felt comfortable with the strategies and could engage in them while paying attention to what the children were doing. In this regard, they recommended that teachers practice the strategies with each other or someone at home. I should have taken this advice before I tried to demonstrate my own strategies. But my rustiness served a purpose. The teachers saw that they needed to practice the procedures before using them with children.

It is important to emphasize that there is nothing hard about presenting the strategies, but no one can become smooth and fluent without some practice. The teachers that I have observed are quite marvelous: they change pace, they watch what the children are doing, they go back several steps if they see that it is necessary, and so on. My recommendation is that it will be to your advantage to do what I suggest, rather than what I recently did!

THERE'S MORE TO IT THAN DECODING

I want to emphasize again that decoding is a necessary but not sufficient condition for becoming a good reader. Being a good reader requires being able to decode and being able to decode automatically—that is, with little overt attention. Additionally, being a good reader also involves knowing the meanings of lots of words and dealing with the ideas in a text. Along with colleagues, I have written about these issues in many other places (e.g., Beck & McKeown, 2001; Beck, McKeown, & Kucan, 2002; McKeown & Beck, 2003). When it comes to developing vocabulary and comprehension for young children a major point is that young children's listening and speaking competence is ahead of their reading competence. That is, they can understand much more from oral language than they can from reading independently. As children are developing their decoding and word-recognition skills, teachers can take advantage of their listening and speaking competence to enhance their vocabulary and comprehension development. Adding vocabulary to children's repertoires and scaffolding their ability to follow a complicated text should not be held back until their word recognition becomes adequate.

First, let's consider vocabulary. In practice, "vocabulary" in the early grades often means providing sight word instruction for high-frequency words (e.g., *give, have, were*). The evidence for this can be found by looking at the kinds of words that are provided in basal reading series under "vocabulary" in the earliest grades. Providing instruction for high-frequency words is essential, but such instruction has nothing to do with helping children develop a treasury of interesting and precise words. Moreover, the words in stories that young children read on their own in the early grades are not sources for adding to children's vocabularies. In the beginning phases of learning to read, children read books that support their developing understanding of how print works. These books make use of simple words, those they already know aurally (e.g., *mom, dog, run*), and that is the way it should be. But as children are learning to recognize in print the words they already know from oral language, they are quite able to learn other kinds of words, words that are interesting and precise and sophisticated (e.g., *extraordinary, journey, dignified*). Such words are used by the authors of tradebooks. But it is not just a matter of reading those books to children. More must go on with some of the words. There are ways to engage children in learning sophisticated words that will allow them to use and indeed enjoy such words (Beck et al., 2002).

Now let's consider comprehension. To develop comprehension, the materials to be comprehended need to be challenging enough so that children have to grapple with ideas and take an active stance toward understanding. Challenging content can be presented to young children from book selections that are read aloud. But it is not just a matter of reading a good story to children. Rather, research indicates that it is the talk about the ideas in the course of hearing a story that is key to read-aloud experiences being valuable for future literacy. Forming ideas about what is in a story and expressing them in ways that make sense to others are ingredients of building literacy competence (McKeown & Beck, 2003; Beck & McKeown, 2005).

COMING FULL CIRCLE

I started this book by talking a bit about 15 first graders, who—in retrospect I likely failed. When I finished a complete draft of the chapters in this book, I took it to another room—far away from my computer—and read it. As I read, one of the questions that came to mind was "If I had been given this book way back then, would I have failed those 15 children?" "I think not!" At a minimum, those who were like the first grader in Chapter 2 (who didn't understand the alphabetic principle) would probably have left first grade at least in the reading ballpark.

Some of the sergeants I taught were not in the reading ballpark when I met them. In particular I remember a young, tall, blond sergeant, who, after he had learned to work his way through words, told me that in the past if he went to a movie alone, he didn't tell his buddies. He explained that if they asked what movie he had seen, he wouldn't have been able to tell them because he couldn't read the name of the movie on the marquee. To this day, I take joy in the fact that the sergeant can now go to the movies on his own.

A different kind of story comes out of a first-grade class in which my colleagues and I were implementing a read-aloud approach. One of the stories, *A Sheepish Tale* (Marshall, 1991), is about two sheep who go for a walk in the woods. One of the sheep claims he can read and announces incorrectly what signs posted in the woods say. His final blunder is reading "pretty green forest" when it actually says "wolf's den." You can imagine how the story goes from there, although the sheep do eventually escape from the wolf. At the conclusion of the story, I was told about a little girl who kept shaking her head back and forth, earnestly saying several times, "See what can happen when you can't read. See what can happen when you can't read." I think that she and the sergeant would have something to talk about.

■ YOUR TURN ■

As a means of considering what might be done for weak readers, think of several students who left your class not reading well. Do you think there is something else you could have done?

Are there strategies in this book that might have been helpful? What are they? Why might they have helped? If you completed the Your Turn at the end of Chapter 2, you might want to review your responses on the basis of ideas you have encountered in this book.

In the area of taking joy in what you have done, think about your influence on several proficient readers in your classroom—past or present. What do you think your contributions were?

CVC Pattern

The 36 A sequences that follow move from simple CVC words (*cat*) to more complex variations of the CVC pattern (*clock, squish*).

The consonants, consonant digraphs, spelling patterns, and short vowels that are included in the A sequences are *first* encountered as shown below. Consonant blends are shown in parentheses (*br*). Note, however, that these letters will be repeated in numerous subsequent sequences

a, d, m, s, t, n, (nd)	Unit 1
i, h	Unit 2
c, o, g	Unit 3
p, f, (st), (sn), (sp)	Unit 4
e	Unit 5
sh, k, ck	Unit 6
b, r, l, (br), (pr), (tr)	Unit 7
u, j	Unit 8
th, (dr), (gr), (sl), (fl), (cl)	Unit 9
ch	Unit 10
w, (sw), (mp)	Unit 11
x, v, qu, (squ), (lt), z	Unit 12

UNIT 1 (A1, A2, A3)

The three sequences below are targeted for the very beginning of instruction, so the content is kept simple. That is, the sequences in Unit 1 are some of the few times that only one vowel, the short-*a* vowel, appears in the sequence. Additionally, in the first sequence, A1, letter changes are only made in the first letter, but in the second and third sequences both initial and final letters are changed. In the third sequence four-letter words are included. Notice that in A3 after children have read *and*, the teacher asks them to put an *s* in front of the *a* and to read the resultant word (*sand*). At the end of the sequence children are asked to put an *s* after the *t* and read *ants*.

A1	A2	A3
dad	sad	at
sad	sat	an
a, d, d, m, s	a, d, d, m, s, t	a, d, n, s, t
mad	mat	ant
dad	mad	and
sad	sad	sand
dad	dad	and
mad	sad	ant
	sat	ants

QUICK CHECK

Child reads	Yes	No	If no, redo
sad			A1
mat			A2
sand			A3

UNIT 2 (A4, A5, A6)

In these three sequences the short *i* appears for the first time and is immediately contrasted with the short *a*. Recall why a new vowel sound is contrasted with previous vowels immediately. As discussed earlier, the vowels are the most difficult elements in English orthography, and children do get them mixed up. As such, it is useful to put children into situations in which they may get mixed up (such as reading *sat* for *sit*) so that instruction can be targeted to what is mixing them up. It is essential that children discriminate among short-vowel grapheme–phoneme correspondences. Also notice that in the last two sequences some consonants are changed in both initial and final position.

A4	A5	A6
sat	hit	ham
sit	hid	him
a, i, s, t	a, d, h, i, s, t	a, d, d, h, i, m, t
sit	hid	ham
sat	had	him
at	sad	hit
it	sat	hid
sit	sit	had
sat	hat	ham
sit	at	him
	it	dim
	hit	did
		dad

QUICK CHECK

Child reads	Yes	No	If no, redo
sit			A4
hid			A5
him			A6
ham			A6

UNIT 3 (A7, A8, A9)

In these three sequences the short *o* is encountered and contrasted with the short *a* in A7. The short *o* is then contrasted with the short *a* and short *i* in A8 and A9. Additionally, notice that in A9 attention is paid to the *g* in final position, which sometimes appears to be a little difficult for beginning readers.

A7	A8	A9
hat	had	dog
hot	hid	dig
a, c, h, n, o, t	a, c, d, h, i, o, t	a, d, g, h, i, o, t
not	had	hit
hot	hid	hot
hat	hit	got
at	hot	dot
cat	hat	dog
cot	cat	dig
hot	cot	dog
not	dot	hog
		hot
		hat
		hit

QUICK CHECK

Child reads	Yes	No	If no, redo
hot			A7
cat			A8
cot			A8
dig			A9
dog			A9

UNIT 4 (A10, A11, A12)

The three sequences in Unit 4 include consonant blends. As noted earlier, consonant blends will appear in a sequence after each of the single consonants that make up a blend have been encountered. Recall the particular value of Word Building for strengthening understanding and responses to, for instance, differences between *snap* and *nap, top* and *stop*. Note the direction for inserting a letter within a word: if you are changing *cat* to *cast,* after *cat* has been read, simply tell the children to move the *t* over and to put the *s* between the *a* and the *t.*

A10	A11	A12
top	fast	cat
stop	fist	can
i, o, p, p, s, t	a, f, i, n, s, t	a, c, n, o, p, s, t
pop	fast	cap
top	fist	tap
stop	fin	nap
top	fan	snap
pop	if	nap
pot	in	cap
spot	fin	cat
spit	fan	cast
pit	fast	cat
pot		cot

QUICK CHECK

Child reads	Yes	No	If no, redo
pop			A10
stop			A10
spot			A10
fast			A11
snap			A12

UNIT 5 (A13, A14, A15)

The short *e* is encountered and first contrasted with the short *a* in A13. In A14, the short *e* is contrasted with the short *o*. Then, in A15, the vowels *e*, *o*, and *a* appear. Note that consonant blends continue to be included when they can produce appropriate words.

A13	A14	A15
stop	ten	pet
step	pen	pot
a, e, n, p, s, t	e, g, n, o, p, s, t	a, e, o, p, s, t
pet	ten	pet
pat	pen	pest
past	pet	pet
pest	pest	pat
nest	pet	pot
net	spot	spot
set	pot	pot
sat	not	pat
pat	net	past
past	get	pat
pest	got	pet
		pest

QUICK CHECK

Child reads	Yes	No	If no, redo
net			A13
pest			A14
past			A15

UNIT 6 (A16, A17, A18)

The emphasis in these sequences are the consonant digraphs *sh* and *ck*. It is important that the two letters in a digraph appear on the same card. In A18, make the point that *k* by itself and *ck* together both represent the /k/ sound. When moving from *stick* to *sick*, ask the children to take the *t* away and move the *s* over to the *i*.

A16	A17	A18
ship	ship	kid
shin	sip	kick
d, f, i, n, p, sh	d, h, i, o, p, s, sh	a, ck, d, i, k, s, sh, t
ship	dip	kid
shin	ship	kick
fin	shop	sick
fish	hop	sack
dish	hip	shack
fish	ship	sack
fin	sip	sash
in	ship	sack
shin	shop	stack
	hop	stick
		sick
		kick

QUICK CHECK

Child reads	Yes	No	If no, redo
fish			A16
shop			A17
kick			A18

UNIT 7 (A19, A20, A21)

The focus in A19 is on *b, r, l,* and *p* because in the two sequences that follow those consonants will be part of consonant blends. As such, the intent is to high- light each of those single consonant grapheme phonemes. The rationale, for example, is that if the *b* to /b/and *l* to /l/relationships are strong, there may be less of a chance that children will omit the phoneme in *black* and read *back* or omit the next-to-last phoneme in *pest* and read *pet,* which, as noted earlier, is what poor readers tend to do.

A19	A20	A21
bag	bag	tick
rag	brag	stick
a, b, e, g, l, p, r, t, s	a, b, ck, g, i, l, m, p, r, t	a, ck, i, p, r, s, t,
peg	rag	tick
beg	brag	tack
leg	bag	stack
lag	back	sack
rag	black	sap
bag	lack	rap
beg	rack	trap
bet	rick	trip
best	brick	trick
rest	brim	track
pest	prim	tack
past	pram	sack
	tram	

QUICK CHECK

Child reads	Yes	No	If no, redo
best			A19
brag			A20
black			A20
trick			A21
stack			A21

UNIT 8 (A22, A23, A24)

In the first sequence below, the short *u* is encountered and contrasted with the short *a*. In the next sequence, the short *u* is contrasted with the short *i*. Then in A24, the vowels *a*, *e*, and *o* appear. Note that in A23, children are asked to exchange one letter card for two, the *g* in *jug* for the *s* and *t* in *just*. The directions are simply to tell the children to take the *g* away and to put the letter *s* next to the *u* and the *t* next to the *s*.

A22	A23	A24
bat but	big bug	rush rash
a, b, f, n, t, u	b, g, i, j, r, s, t, u,	a, c, o, p, r, sh, t, u
fun fan fat bat but tub tab bat but nut	but bit big jig jug just bust but rut rub rib	cash rash rush cut shut cut cup cop shop top

QUICK CHECK

Child reads	Yes	No	If no, redo
fun bust rush			A22 A23 A24

UNIT 9 (A25, A26, A27)

The focus in A25 is the *th* digraph. The second and third sequences include the first encounter of five high-frequency consonant blends: *dr, gr, sl, fl, cl.*

A25	A26	A27
path thin	tap trap	slip flip
a, b, i, n, p, t, th	a, d, g, i, n, p, r, t	a, c, f, i, l, o, p, s
pin pan path bath path pat pit pin thin	trip drip rip grip grin in an and grand	flop flap slap lap lip flip slip clip

QUICK CHECK

Child reads	Yes	No	If no, redo
thin trip grip flop slap clip			A25 A26 A26 A27 A27 A27

UNIT 10 (A28, A29, A30)

In A28 the *ch* digraph is encountered. The focus in A29 is the *ck*. A30 includes both *ch* and *ck* words so that children experience the difference between the two units.

A28	A29	A30
chip chin	lick click	check peck
ch, i, l, m, n, p, u	a, c, ck, i, l, o, s, t	a, ch, ck, e, h, n, p, t
chip chin in inch pinch punch lunch munch much	lick lock clock sock sick stick stack stock clock click lick	check peck pen pan pat chat hat hatch hat pat pack pat patch

QUICK CHECK

Child reads	Yes	No	If no, redo
chip			A28
much			A28
clock			A29
peck			A30
check			A30

UNIT 11 (A31, A32, A33)

The *w* is encountered in A31 and the consonant blend *sw* in A32. The last sequence, A33, focuses on the *mp* in the final position. Notice the usefulness of bringing attention to the *mp* by changing *lamp* to *lap* and *lip* to *limp*.

A31	A32	A33
with	wing	lip
wig	swing	lamp
a, d, g, i, sh, th, w	a, g, i, m, n, s, sh, t, th, w	a, i, l, m, p, s, t, u
wish	wing	stamp
with	win	stump
wish	twin	lump
dish	thin	lamp
dash	win	lap
dish	wish	lip
wish	with	limp
wig	wish	lip
wag	swish	lap
wig	swim	lamp
with	swam	limp
wish	swan	

QUICK CHECK

Child reads	Yes	No	If no, redo
wish			A31
swim			A32
lump			A33

UNIT 12 (A34, A35, A36)

The consonant *x* is encountered in A34 and the consonants *v* and *z* are encountered in A35. A36 focuses on *qu*, and includes the blends *squ* and *lt*.

A34	A35	A36
fix	vet	quick
fox	van	quilt
a, b, f, i, m, o, s, x	a, b, e, n, s, t, v	a, ck, i, l, n, qu, s, sh, t, z
box	van	quit
ox	vat	quiz
ax	bat	quick
max	bet	quit
mix	vet	squint
six	vest	squish
fix	best	squash
fox	nest	quilt
box	vest	quit
	vast	quiz

QUICK CHECK

Child reads	Yes	No	If no, redo
mix			A34
vest			A35
quit			A36

Long Vowels of the CVCe Pattern

The 15 B sequences that follow deal with long vowels of the CVCe pattern (i.e., *made*). When possible CVCe patterns are introduced by initially providing a known CVC (i.e., *man*) and then contrasting its corresponding CVCe (i.e., *mane*).

The patterns are encountered in the following order: *ate, ane, ake, ape,* etc.

UNIT 13 (B1, B2, B3)

The focus of this unit is the CaCe (consonant, vowel **a**, consonant, silent e) pattern. Known CVCs are changed to CaCes by adding the silent e, and changed back to CVCs by removing the silent e. In B1, students encounter the **a**Ces: *ate, ane,* and *ake,* which are included in subsequent sequences as appropriate. In B2, *ape, ade,* and *ame* are included. In the third sequence, B3, the CaCe patterns appear in words that include consonant blends.

B1	B2	B3
can	mate	grape
cane	make	grate
a, c, e, k, m, n, r, t	a, d, e, g, k, m, n, p, t	a, e, g, l, m, n, p, r, s, t
mat	gate	gate
mate	gape	grate
mat	gap	rate
man	tap	ate
mane	tape	plate
cane	tap	plane
can	tam	lane
ran	tame	late
rat	make	slate
rate	made	slam
rake	mad	slap
make	man	lap
cake	pan	tap
take	pane	tape

QUICK CHECK

Child reads	Yes	No	If no, redo
make			B1
mad			B2
made			B2
grape			B3
plate			B3

UNIT 14 (B4, B5, B6)

The first two sequences in this unit, B4 and B5, focus on the C**o**Ce (consonant, vowel **o**, consonant, silent e). In B4, students encounter the **o**Ces ope and obe, which are included in subsequent sequences as appropriate. In B5, the focus is on ope, ole, and ode. B6 includes both C**o**Ce and C**a**Ce patterns.

B4	B5	B6
cop	hope	cope
cope	hop	cape
b, c, e, l, m, o, p, r, s, t	c, d, e, h, l, m, o, p, r	a, c, e, f, h, k, l, o, p, t
cop	hope	hop
cope	mope	hope
slope	mop	cope
slop	hop	cape
stop	hope	cap
top	cope	tap
mop	code	tape
mope	rode	take
rope	role	fake
robe	pole	flake
rob	mole	lake
robe	mope	fate
rope	mop	fat

QUICK CHECK

Child reads	Yes	No	If no, redo
rope			B4
mole			B5
hope			B5
take			B6
cape			B6

UNIT 15 (B7, B8, B9)

The first two sequences in this unit, B7 and B8, focus on the CiCe pattern. Students will encounter *ime, ide, ine, ive,* and *ipe*. As appropriate, those patterns will continue to be compared to CVC patterns. The third sequence, B9, includes CiCe, CoCe and CaCe patterns.

B7	B8	B9
slid	dime	hid
slide	dive	hide
d, e, h, i, l, m, r, s,	d, e, f, i, l, m, n, p, r, t, v	a, d, e, h, i, m, n, o, p, r
dim	fine	hid
dime	fin	rid
dim	fine	ride
him	five	rode
hid	fine	ride
hide	dine	hide
side	dime	hid
sid	dim	had
slid	dime	mad
slide	time	made
slid	tim	mad
lid	tip	man
rid	rip	mane
ride	ripe	mine
		pine
		pin

QUICK CHECK

Child reads	Yes	No	If no, redo
hide			B7
five			B8
dime			B8
rode			B9
made			B9

UNIT 16 (B10, B11, B12)

The first two sequences in this unit, B10 and B11, focus on the C**u**Ce pattern and continue to compare it to CVC patterns. The third sequence, B12, includes C**u**Ce and C**o**Ce patterns.

B10	B11	B12
cut	tub	note
cute	tube	not
b, c, e, m, r, t, u	b, c, e, f, m, n, t, u	c, e, l, m, n, o, p, s, t, u
cut	tub	note
mut	tube	not
mute	cube	nut
mut	cub	cut
cut	cut	cute
cute	cute	mute
cube	mute	mut
cub	mut	cut
cube	but	cot
tube	bun	cop
tub	fun	cope
rub	run	slope
cub		slop
cube		lop
		cop

QUICK CHECK

Child reads	Yes	No	If no, redo
cute			B10
but			B11
cube			B11
cot			B12
slope			B12

UNIT 17 (B13, B14, B15)

This unit focuses on the soft *c* in Ci**C**e and Ca**C**e patterns. The soft *c* is quite prevalent in *ace* and *ice* words.

B13	B14	B15
rice race	mile mice	pin pine
a, c, e, f, i, n, n, m, p, r	a, c, e, i, l, m, n, p, r, s, t	a, c, e, i, k, l, n, p, s, t
race face race rice price rice nice nine mine mice ice ace pace	mile mice nice spice spine pin pine pace space pace place race trace rice price	pin pan pane pace lace place ace ice slice spice space spike like lake late lace place

QUICK CHECK

Child reads	Yes	No	If no, redo
race nice space place ice			B13 B13 B14 B15 B15

Long-Vowel Digraph Patterns

The 15 C sequences deal with long-vowel digraph patterns. Students will encounter different combinations of letters that represent the same sound. It is important that students explicitly be told that sometimes different letters stand for the same sound. Also in the C sequences, students will sometimes be asked to change more than one letter at a time.

The long patterns in the C sequences include:

long *e* as in *seat* and *seed*
long *a* as in *rain* and *day*
long *o* as in *goat* and *grow*
long *u* as in *clue* and *crew*

UNIT 18 (C1, C2, C3)

In C1, words with *ee* and *ea* are encountered. Before you begin C1, place the words *seat* and *seed* under one another and tell students that the letters *ea* represent the /e/ sound in *seat* and that the letters *ee* represent the /e/ sound in *seed*. When you get to homophones (*sea* and *see*) tell students that *sea* means a huge body of water and that *see* means what we do with our eyes. When you change *need* to *neat*, students need to change two letter cards. Direct students to remove both *ee* and *d*. Then put *ea* after *n* and put *t* at the end of the word. In C2, *ea* long-*e* words are contrasted with short-*e* and short-*a* words. C2 and C3 include *ee, ea,* short-*e,* and short-*a* words.

C1	C2	C3
seat	sat	net
seed	seat	neat
d, ea, ee, m, n, s, t	a, e, ea, h, s, t	a, d, e, ea, ee, n, s, t
meat	sat	net
eat	seat	neat
seat	sea	eat
sea*	seat	seat
see*	sat	sat
seed	set	set
need	seat	seat
neat	eat	sea
seat	at	see
sea	sat	seed
see	seat	need
	heat	needs

*Explain the difference.

QUICK CHECK

Child reads	Yes	No	If no, redo
neat			C1
seed			C1
set			C2
seat			C4

UNIT 19 (C4, C5, C6)

The first two sequences (C4 and C5) deal with the *ai* digraph, which is contrasted with the short *a*. In C6, the CaCe Pattern is included along with *ai* and short-*a* words.

C4	C5	C6
ran	pad	man
rain	paid	mane
a, ai, m, n, p, r, t	a, ai, d, m, n, p	a, ai, d, e, m, n, p
pain	pad	made
pan	pan	mad
man	pain	man
main	main	main
man	man	man
ran	mad	pan
rain	maid	pad
train	main	paid
rain	pain	pad
ran	pan	pan
pan		pane
pain		pan
		pain

QUICK CHECK

Child reads	Yes	No	If no, redo
pain			C4
mad			C5
made			C6
main			C6

UNIT 20 (C7, C8, C9)

In C7, the *ay* digraph is encountered and contrasted with the short *a*. In C8, the *ai* digraph is encountered and both the *ay* and *ai* digraphs are included. Then in C9, the long-*a* sound as represented in C**a**Ce patterns and the *ay* and *ai* digraphs are included. Again notice that in each of these sequences there will be times when students need to change two letter cards.

C7	C8	C9
pan pay	may main	main made
a, ay, l, m, n, p, r, t	a, ai, ay, b, d, l, m, n, p, t	a, ai, ay, d, e, m, n, p, t
may man pan pay pan ran ray tray ray lay play lay ray	pay paid maid laid lad bad bat bait bat bait maid mad may main man	pay pain pan man mad made mad mat mate mat mad maid main man may

QUICK CHECK

Child reads	Yes	No	If no, redo
pay main may made			C7 C8 C9 C9

UNIT 21 (C10, C11, C12)

In C10, the *oa* digraph is encountered and contrasted with the short *o*. In C11, the *ow* digraph appears and is contrasted with the short *o*. Then in C12 both the *ow* and *oa* digraphs are included. As in the other units, there will be instances where two letter cards are changed.

C10	C11	C12
got goat	lot low	low load
c, d, g, k, l, n, o, oa, r, s, t, t	b, g, l, o, t, ow, r, s	b, d, g, l, m, n, oa, ow, r, t
got goat road rod road roast toast toad load loan oak soak cloak	lob low slow glow low lot blot blow low lot rot row grow	loan groan grown grow row road toad tow mow moat bow

QUICK CHECK

Child reads	Yes	No	If no, redo
goat slow load low			C10 C11 C12 C12

UNIT 22 (C13, C14, C15)

These sequences deal with the long *u* as represented in *ew* and *ue*. In C13, after you build *blew* and *blue*, display the words—one under the other—and explain that *blew* is what the wind did and *blue* is the color. In these sequences minimal contrasts of the vowel are not possible. As such, the sequences are kept short and provide students with a quick introduction to or review of the patterns. Notice that in C15 students must take all cards away except one. For instance, when *grew* is to be changed to *glue* the direction will be to take all the letters except the *g* away and then to put *l*, *u*, and *e* after the *g*.

C13	C14	C15
few stew	cue blue	blew blue
c, d, ew, f, n, r, s, sh, t, th	b, c, d, g, h, l, ue, s	b, c, ch, d, ew, g, l, r, ue
dew drew new few screw shrew stew threw	glue blue clue cue sue due hue	grew glue clue cue crew chew dew drew due

QUICK CHECK

Child reads	Yes	No	If no, redo
stew			C13
cue			C14
grew			C15
glue			C15

r-Controlled Digraph Patterns

The nine D sequences deal with some *r*-controlled vowel patterns. Students will encounter different combinations of letters that represent the same sound. It is important that students explicitly be told that sometimes different letters stand for the same sound. Also in the D sequences, students will sometimes be asked to change more than one letter at a time.

The *r*-controlled patterns in the D sequences include:

ar as in *star*
or as in *born*
ir as in *bird*
er as in *stern*
ur as in *turn*

UNIT 23 (D1, D2, D3)

The three sequences in this unit deal with the *ar-* and *or-* vowel-controlled patterns. In D1, students deal with the *ar*. In D2, students encounter the *or* pattern, and in D3 both the *ar* and *or* patterns are included. As was the case with vowel digraphs in the C sequences, it is important to tell students which two letters together produce a phoneme (i.e., in D1, the *ar* letters together represent the /ar/ sound in *start*).

D1	**D2**	**D3**
star	sport	car
cart	port	tar
ar, c, d, f, k, m, p, s, t	f, k, n, or, p, s, t,	ar, c, f, k, or, s, t
art	fort	star
arm	torn	far
farm	sort	for
far	for	fork
car	fork	stork
cart	fort	stark
dart	port	star
dark	sport	car
mark		cart
spark		
park		
part		

QUICK CHECK

Child reads	Yes	No	If no, redo
farm			D1
port			D2
stark			D3
stork			D3

UNIT 24 (D4, D5, D6)

In D4, the *er* pattern appears. In D5, the *ir* pattern is encountered, and in D6, both *er* and *ir* are included. (It is important to tell students when two sets of letters can represent the same phoneme.) For example, in D6 after having made *fern* and *firm*, the teacher should place the two words under one another and tell students that in the word *sir* the letters *ir* together make the /er/ sound and in the word *her* the letters *er* together also make the /er/ sound.

D4	D5	D6
her herd	bird birth	fern firm
c, d, er, h, j, k, l, p	b, d, f, ir, k, m, s, t, th	d, er, f, h, ir, m, n, s, t
her herd clerk per perk jerk clerk herd	bird third thirst first firm fir sir stir skirt dirt smirk irk	fern firm fir stir stern fern her herd

QUICK CHECK

Child reads	Yes	No	If no, redo
herd skirt stir stern			D4 D5 D6 D6

UNIT 25 (D7, D8, D9)

In D7, the *ur* pattern appears. In D8, the *ur, er* and *ir* are encountered. In D9, *ar, er, ir, or* and *ur* are included. (It is important to tell students when two sets of letters can represent the same phoneme.)

D7	D8	D9
fur hurt	burn bird	dart dirt
b, ch, f, h, l, n, t, ur	b, d, er, f, h, ir, n, s, t, th, ur	ar, d, er, f, ir, m, n, or, s, t, ur
fur turn burn churn burn burnt hurt blur blurt hurt hurl churn	burn hurt her herd bird fir sir stir stern fern first burst thirst	fir for far firm form storm stir stern turn torn tar turf surf stern

QUICK CHECK

Child reads	Yes	No	If no, redo
turn stir storm stern surf			D7 D8 D9 D9 D9

Word and Syllable Matrices for Syllasearch

There are three sets of words and syllable matrices for Syllasearch. The Easy Set includes only two-syllable words. The Medium Set includes both two- and three-syllable words, and the Hard Set includes two-, three-, and four-syllable words.

EASY SET

	Words	Syllables	
1.	funny	fun	ty
	penny	pen	cle
	forgive	cir	ny
	circle	par	cus
	circus	for	lor
	parlor		give
	party		
	forty		
2.	puppy	pup	tion
	puppet	hap	tor
	happy	mo	pet
	happen	gig	py
	motor	wig	pen
	motion		gle
	giggle		
	wiggle		
3.	barber	pil	ware
	barter	be	long
	beware	fol	ter
	belong	shal	ber
	below	bar	low
	follow		
	pillow		
	shallow		

(continued)

Words	Syllables	
4.		
bottle	bot	dent
bottom	lit	tom
little	stu	tle
cattle	in	pid
order	cat	der
student	or	
stupid		
indent		
5.		
apple	ap	con
applaud	tram	plaud
trample	ba	ple
bacon	for	by
baby	ma	est
forest		get
forget		
maple		
6.		
dollar	dol	lect
collar	col	lar
collect	mum	lege
college	de	ble
mumble	peb	part
delight		light
depart		
pebble		
7.		
perhaps	per	row
person	les	fect
perfect	nar	age
lesson	pack	haps
narrow	bor	son
borrow	stor	
storage		
package		

(continued)

Words	Syllables	
8.	letter	let	tic
	plastic	at	tach
	plaster	but	ter
	attic	plas	tend
	attend		tempt
	attach		
	attempt		
	butter		
9.	excuse	ex	ic
	explain	com	da
	complain	pan	cuse
	comic		plain
	command		mand
	panic		
	panda		

MEDIUM SET

Words	Syllables		
1. family	fam	i	mal
suddenly	sud	ful	ly
sudden	an	den	er
another	help	oth	
animal	hid		
helpful			
helpfully			
hidden			
2. picnic	pic	der	ful
picture	pow	ture	ble
powder	vis	nic	tor
power	nev	i	
powerful		er	
visitor			
visible			
never			
3. principal	prin	tion	dent
princess	re	ci	pal
return	ac	turn	
accident	na	cess	
nation			
recess			
action			
access			

(continued)

Words	Syllables		
4. center	cen	ket	ous
market	mar	ter	lade
marvel	bris	vel	
marvelous	chap	shal	
marshal		ma	
marmalade			
brisket			
chapter			
5. comfort	com	tack	tion
commotion	rot	fort	dance
attention	at	ten	
attendance	pur	mo	
purchase	kit	sue	
pursue		chase	
kitten			
rotten			
attack			
6. hollow	yes	bust	tial
holiday	hol	i	day
yesterday	ro	dent	
robust	in	ter	
rodent		struct	
indent		low	
initial			
instruct			
7. person	gen	fect	man
complete	per	tle	ment
travel	com	vel	
compartment	sho	son	
gentleman	tra	part	
perfect		plete	
shovel			
gentle			

(continued)

	Words	Syllables		
8.	vacation	can	yon	tion
	improve	va	ca	ment
	improvement	dis	prove	
	immense	im	play	
	cancel		mense	
	canyon		cel	
	disprove			
	display			
9.	become	be	ware	tion
	beware	a	come	
	income	in	lec	
	aware	se	date	
	alert	e	cure	
	selection		lert	
	sedate			
	secure			
	election			
10.	discover	dis	cov	er
	distract	re	tract	cal
	contract	prac	tire	
	consider	ver	ti	
	retract	con	sid	
	retire			
	practical			
	vertical			
11.	interrupt	in	ter	rupt
	invent	pre	vent	view
	interview	cra	dle	
	prevent	de	vour	
	cradle	rid		
	crater			
	deter			
	devour			
	riddle			

(continued)

Words	Syllables		
12. alphabet	al	fec	bet
alibi	in	i	tion
album	ad	pha	bi
infection		bum	tage
admire		mit	
advantage		mire	
admit		van	
alpha			
13. exam	ex	cel	ple
example	can	tial	lent
excellent	par	am	
excel		lor	
parcel			
parlor			
partial			
cancel			

HARD SET

Words	Syllables			
1. protective	de	mol	ish	
reverse	pro	form	tive	
demolish	re	verse		
detective		ceive		
deform		tec		
deceive				
reform				
receive				

2. authentic	au	then	tic	
audible	ca	pa	ble	
audition	gi	di	tion	
capable	tra	tumn		
cater		ter		
autumn		gan		
gigantic				
tradition				

3. conversation	con	ver	sa	tion
consult	ad	vise	tise	
advertise	fe	sult	dent	
confident	in	just		
advise		fi		
adjust				
fever				
insult				

(continued)

Words	Syllables			
4. accompany	ac	tac	pa	ny
accomplish	mat	tress	plish	lar
spectacular	cap	com	u	
actress	cur	sule		
mattress	spec	tain		
curtain				
captain				
capsule				

5. recreation	rec	tang	le	tion
rectangle	mod	re	a	
simplify	sim	i	lar	
similar	cav	pli	fy	
modify		el	ty	
model		ern		
modern				
cavern				
cavity				

6. addition	ad	stant	tion
adventure	con	form	ture
constant	in	ven	
conform		di	
invention			
condition			
convention			
instant			
inform			

7. procrastinate	pro	crast	in	ate
produce	re	duce	vi	
reduce	ab	bre	ble	
abbreviate	pos	ture	vate	
posture	cul	si		
possible		ti		
culture				
cultivate				

(continued)

Words	Syllables		
8. enrage	en	cour	age
encourage	dis	rage	pear
discourage	sur	ap	
disappear	com	prise	
compress		vive	
comprise		press	
surprise			
survive			

9. profile	res	tect	dent
protect	ev	nounce	due
evident	an	file	
resident	pres	noy	
residue	pro	i	
president			
annoy			
announce			
pronounce			

10. inhabit	home	stant	it
demolish	in	hale	ish
forward	de	form	
homeward	for	hab	
deform		mol	
inward		ward	
instant			
inhale			
inform			

(continued)

	Words	Syllables			
11.	hesitate	van	tinct	tate	
	resume	pre	sume	ty	
	vanity	re	i		
	preserve	hes	tend		
	extinct	ex	serve		
	extend				
	pretend				
	presume				
	reserve				
12.	remarkable	re	mark	a	ble
	propel	ex	li	ler	
	propeller	pro	cel		
	remark		pel		
	reliable				
	repel				
	expel				
	excel				

The Word Pocket

A Word Pocket is simply a one-row pocket into which a child can place letters to make a word. To make a Word Pocket use a 12-by-9-inch sheet of tag board. On the 12-inch dimension, mark and score a line 1 inch from the bottom and fold along the line to make a pocket. Staple the ends.

The advantage of the Word Pocket is that it helps to show the earliest learners where the beginning, middle, and end letters in a word belong. Some teachers put a green dot (as a "go" sign) at the very left of the Word Pocket to show where the first letter of a word belongs. As children become familiar with building words, which they do quite rapidly, most teachers have found that they can simply build their words on their desks.

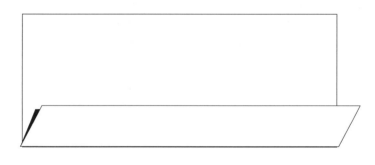

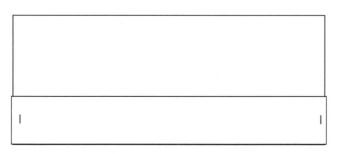

Lowercase letter cards that can be duplicated and are appropriate for a 12-by-9-inch Word Pocket follow.

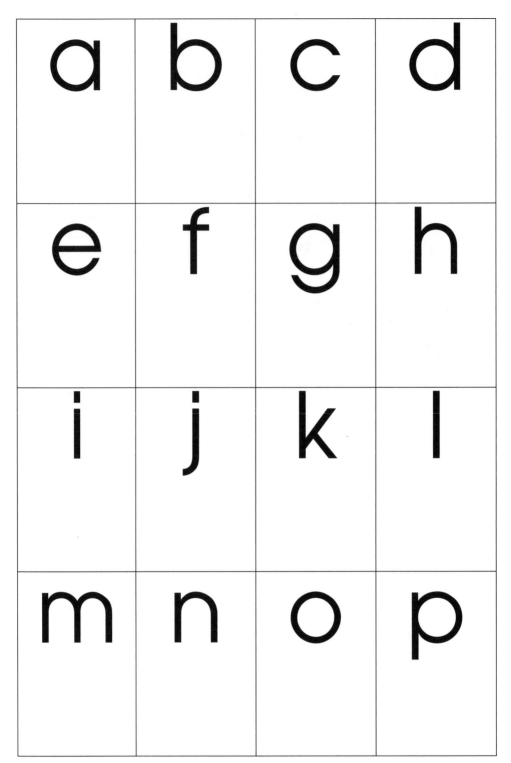

From *Making Sense of Phonics* by Isabel L. Beck. Copyright 2006 by The Guilford Press. Permission to photocopy this material is granted to purchasers of this book for personal use only (see copyright page for details).

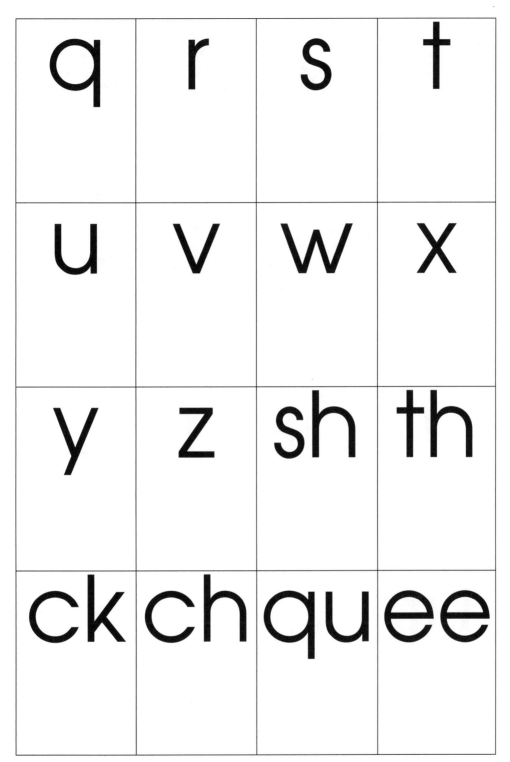

q	r	s	t
u	v	w	x
y	z	sh	th
ck	ch	qu	ee

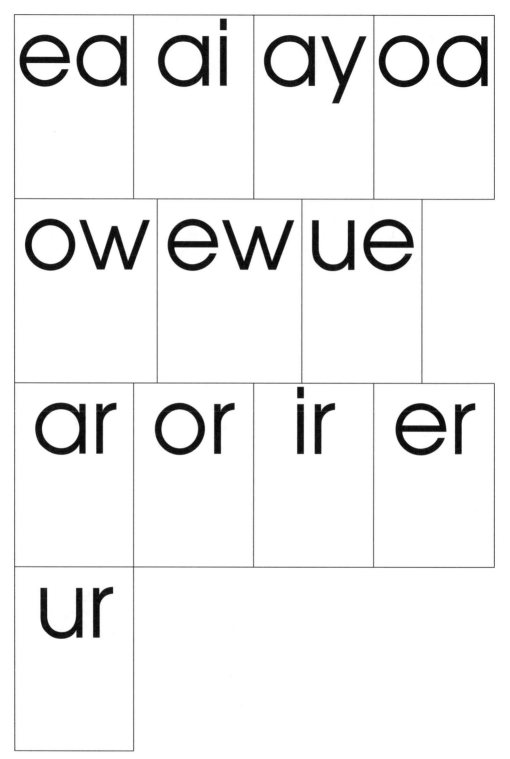

ea	ai	ay	oa
ow	ew	ue	
ar	or	ir	er
ur			

REFERENCES

Adams, M. J., & Bruck, M. (1995). Resolving the "Great Debate." *American Educator, 19*(2), 7–20.

Armbruster, B. B., Lehr, F., & Osborn, J. (2001). *Put reading first: The research building blocks for teaching children to read*. Washington, DC: Center for the Improvement of Early Reading Achievement.

Beck, I. L. (1998). Understanding beginning reading: A journey through teaching and research. In J. Osborn & F. Lehr (Eds.), *Literacy for all: Issues in teaching and learning* (pp. 11–31). New York: Guilford Press.

Beck, I. L., & Hamilton, R. (1996). *Beginning reading module*. Developed for the Education Research and Development Program of the American Federation of Teachers. A workshop of this module was presented at the 1996 Winter Institute in Baltimore, MD.)

Beck, I. L., & McCaslin, E. S. (1978). *An analysis of dimensions that affect the development of code-breaking ability in eight beginning reading programs* (LRDC Publication No. 1978/6). Pittsburgh, PA: University of Pittsburgh, Learning Research and Development Center.

Beck, I. L., & McKeown, M. G., (2001). Text Talk: Capturing the benefits of read-aloud experiences for young children. *The Reading Teacher, 55* (1), 10–20.

Beck, I. L., & McKeown, M. G. (2005). Encouraging young children's language interactions with stories. In D. K. Dickinson, & S. B. Neuman (Eds.), *Handbook of early literacy research* (Vol. 2, pp. 281–294). New York: Guilford Press.

Beck I. L., McKeown, M. G., & Kucan, L. (2002). *Bringing words to life: Robust vocabulary instruction*. New York: Guilford Press.

Beck, I. L., & Mitroff, D. D. (1972). *The rationale and design of a primary grades reading system for an individualized classroom*. (LRDC Publication No. 1972/4). Pittsburgh, PA: University of Pittsburgh, Learning Research and Development Center.

Beck, I. L., Roth, S. F., & McKeown, M. G. (1985). *Syllasearch*. Allen, TX: Developmental Learning Materials.

Bentin, S., & Leshem, H. (1993). On the interaction between phonological awareness and reading acquisition: It's a two-way street. *Annals of Dyslexia, 43,* 125–148.

Bishop, C. H. (1964). Transfer effects of word and letter training in reading. *Journal of Verbal Learning and Verbal Behavior, 3,* 215–221.

Bus, A. G., & Vam IJzendoorn, M. H. (1999). Phonological awareness and early reading: A meta-analysis of experimental training studies. *Journal of Experimental Psychology, 91,* 403–414.

Chall, J. (1967). *Learning to read: The great debate*. New York: McGraw-Hill.

Clay, M. M. (1979). *Reading: The patterning of complex behavior*. Auckland, New Zealand: Heinemann Educational Books.

Ehri, L. C. (1991). Learning to read and spell words. In L. Rieben & C. A. Perfetti (Eds.), *Learning to read: Basic research and its implications* (pp. 57–73). Hillsdale, NJ: Erlbaum.

Ehri, L. C. (1999). Phases of development in learning to read words. In J. Oakhill & R. Beard (Eds.), *Reading development and the teaching of reading: A psychological perspective* (pp. 79–108). Oxford, UK: Blackwell.

Flack, M., & Wiese, K. (1933). *The story about Ping*. New York: Viking Press.

Gough, P. B., & Hillinger, M. L. (1980). Learning to read: An un-natural act. *Bulletin of the Orton Society, 30,* 179–196.

Gray, W. S., Monroe, M., Artely, A. S., Arbuthnot, A. H., & Gray, L. (1956). *The new basic readers: Curriculum foundation series*. Chicago: Scott Foresman.

Hurford, D. P., Schauf, J. D., Bunce, L., Blaich, T., & Moore, K. (1994). Early identification of children at risk for reading disabilities. *Journal of Learning Disabilities, 27,* 371–382.

Juel, C. (1988). Learning to read and write: A longitudinal study of fifty-four children from first through fourth grade. *Journal of Educational Psychology, 80,* 437–447.

Juel, C., & Roper-Schneider, D. (1985). The influence of basal readers on first grade reading. *Reading Research Quarterly, 22,* 134–152.

Just, M. A., & Carpenter, P. A. (1987). *The psychology of reading and language comprehension*. Boston: Allyn & Bacon.

Kiss, G. R., & Savage, J. E. (1977). Processing power and delay limits on human performance. *Journal of Mathematical Psychology, 16,* 68–90.

Liberman, I. Y., & Shankweiler, D. (1979). Speech, the alphabet, and teaching to read. In L. B. Resnick & P. A. Weaver (Eds.), *Theory and practice of early reading* (Vol. 2, pp. 109–132). Hillsdale, NJ: Erlbaum.

Mason, J. M., Anderson, R. C., Omura, A., Uchida, N., & Imai, M. (1989). Learning to read in Japan. *Journal of Curriculum Studies, 21,* 389–407.

Marshall, J. (1991). A sheepish tale. In *Rats on the roof and other stories* (pp. 19–28). New York: Puffin Books.

McCandliss, B., Beck, I. L., Sandak, R., & Perfetti, C. (2003). Focusing attention on decoding for children with poor reading skills: Design and preliminary tests of the Word Building intervention. *Scientific Studies of Reading, 7*(1), 75–104.

McCloskey, R. (1941). *Make way for ducklings*. New York: Viking Press.

McKeown, M. G., & Beck, I. L. (2003). Taking advantage of read alouds to help children make sense of decontextualized language. In A. van Kleeck, S. A. Stahl, & E. B. Bauer (Eds.), *Storybook reading* (pp. 159–176). Mahwah, NJ: Erlbaum.

Morais, J., Cary, L., Alegria, J., & Bertelson, P. (1979). Does awareness of speech as a sequence of phones arise spontaneously? *Cognition, 7,* 323–331.

National Reading Panel. (2000). *Teaching children to read: An evidence-based assessment of the scientific literature on reading and its implications for reading instruction*. (NIH Publication No. 00-4754). Washington, DC: National Institutes of Health.

Perfetti, C. A. (1985). *Reading Ability*. New York: Oxford University Press.

Perfetti, C. A. (1992). The representation problem in reading acquisition. In P. B. Gough, L. C. Ehri, & R. Treiman (Eds.), *Reading acquisition* (pp. 145–174). Hillsdale, NJ: Erlbaum.

Perfetti, C. A., & Zhang, S. (1996). What it means to learn to read. In M. F. Graves, B. M. Taylor, & P. van den Broek (Eds.), *The first R: Every child's right to read* (pp. 37–61). New York: Teachers College Press.

Share, D. L. (1995). Phonological recoding and self-teaching: Sine qua non of reading acquisition. *Cognition, 55,* 151–218.

Share, D. L., & Stanovich, K. E. (1995). Cognitive processes in early reading development: Accommodating individual differences into a model of acquisition. *Issues in Education, 1,* 1–57.

Shaywitz, B. A., Shaywitz, S. E., Blachman, B. A., Pugh, K. R., Fulbright, R. K., Skudlarski, P., Mencl, W. E., Constable, R. T., Holahan, J. M., Marchione, K. E., Fletcher, J. M., Lyon, G. R., & Gore, J. C. (2004). Development of left occipitotemporal systems for skilled reading in children after a phonologically based intervention. *Biological Psychiatry, 55,* 926–933.

Shaywitz, S. E., Shaywitz, B. A., Fulbright, R. K., Skudlarski, P., Mencl, W. E., Constable, R. T., Pugh, K. R., Holahan, J. M., Marchione, K. E., Fletcher, J. M., Lyon, G. R., & Gore, J. C. (2003). Neural systems for compensation and persistence: Young adult outcome of childhood reading disability. *Biological Psychiatry, 54,* 25–33.

Stanovich, K. E. (1986). Matthew effects in reading: Some consequences of individual differences in the acquisition of literacy. *Reading Research Quarterly, 21,* 360–406.

INDEX